DATE DUE

Oliver Cromwell

Oliver Cromwell

C. V. Wedgwood

BARNES
&NOBLE
B O O K S
N E W   Y O R K

A. S. P.

in memoriam

Original edition first published 1939
This revised augmented edition copyright © 1973 by C. V. Wedgwood
All rights reserved.

This edition published by Barnes & Noble, Inc.,
by arrangement with Deborah Owen ltd.

1994 Barnes & Noble Books

ISBN 1-56619-549-7

Printed and bound in the United States of America

M 9 8 7 6 5 4 3 2 1

Contents

Oliver Cromwell

ONE

The First Forty Years
1599-1639

'IN the year of Our Lord 1599, Oliver, the son of Robert Cromwell, gentleman, and of Elizabeth his wife, born on the 25th day of April and baptised on the 29th of the same month.' With this formula, in a simplified Latin, the Register Book of the Church of St. John the Baptist at Huntingdon records the birth of the Great Protector.

Oliver Cromwell was four generations removed from a Putney brewer of Welsh origin named Morgan Williams, who had married Katherine, elder sister of Thomas Cromwell. Their son, Richard, adopted the surname of his powerful uncle, and acquired considerable property in East Anglia through the plunder of the monasteries. Richard's son and Oliver's grandfather, Sir Henry Cromwell of Hinchinbrook, and the head of the family in 1599, was commonly known as the 'Golden Knight', and reckoned among the richest men in the district. The bulk of Sir Henry's estates would pass in time to his eldest son. Robert, one of the younger children, had been established in independent possession of a small property at Huntingdon. He had married a widow, Elizabeth Lynn, daughter of Sir William Steward, farmer of the tithes of Ely Cathedral, a solid and sensible woman of a Norfolk family which claimed an improbable connection with the Stuart Kings.

Cromwell was thus of mixed ancestry – Welsh and Anglo-Saxon. At a superficial view, the Anglo-Saxon characteristics seem predominant. In maturity he would be a man of much practical sense, not given to theories, basing his judgments on the facts as he saw them, cautious in decision but resolute in action. Yet there were contradictory elements in his character – a recurrent tendency to melancholia, cured only by an intense religious faith which transformed his smouldering discontent into a prophetic fire, blazing out against all obstacles, so that he would feel himself possessed, a chosen instrument of God.

Nothing survives from Cromwell's childhood, save a few isolated facts, some doubtful legend and much spiteful gossip. As soon as he was old enough, he was sent to the Free School attached to the Hospital of St. John at Huntingdon. The headmaster, Doctor Thomas Beard, was a ferocious Puritan who believed that the Pope was Anti-Christ, and had translated from the French, in a work entitled *The Theatre of God's Judgements*, a stupendous collection of miraculous punishments summarily inflicted by the Almighty on transgressors. He imbued his pupils with faith in, and fear of, a God who neither overlooked nor forgave the shortcomings of his unhappy creation. In this faith Cromwell was to live and die. But as a schoolmaster Dr. Beard did not apparently emulate the vindictive conduct which he admired in Jehovah; the affection and respect which he inspired in Cromwell indicate that, although he may have been stern, he was not unsympathetic.

In his seventeenth year Cromwell was removed from school, and on 23 April 1616 entered at Sidney Sussex College, Cambridge. The Master at this time was the introspective and meticulous Doctor Samuel Ward, under whom the college was fast becoming a nursery for Puritan doctrine. Cromwell himself was placed under the care of a mild little man not very much older than himself, the Reverend Richard Howlett.

At this period legend – which embellishes the sober history of Cromwell's childhood with such tales as that a monkey stole him from his cradle, that he dreamed he was to be King, that he knocked down the infant Charles I in play – becomes vociferous once again. At Cambridge, so Cromwell's enemies later declared, he had passed his time drinking, whoring, playing football and utterly neglecting his studies. Cromwell himself thickened the fog which obscures this early part of his life by dismissing all his youth in the one sentence: 'I lived in and loved darkness and hated the light: I was a chief, the chief, of sinners.' To judge by parallel statements made by religious converts, these dreadful words probably mean very little. At Cambridge he doubtless worked as little and amused himself as much as the young men of his time, which is to say that he worked more and played less than the average undergraduate of to-day. He was a normal young man, clumsily but vigorously built, with a keen taste for outdoor sports, for hawking, hunting and games, which he never outgrew. Tales of his early debaucheries are unsubstantiated, and in the absence of all evidence it may be safely assumed that in his youth he was neither monster nor saint. His gifts were certainly not academic, and in after life his letters and speeches. have a confused effective vigour which owes little to any training in conventional rhetoric. But he remembered enough Latin to converse with foreign ambassadors, which is evidence that he cannot wholly have neglected his books.

He left Cambridge without a degree, little more than a year after his first coming, for no other reason than the sudden death of his father. A legal quibble made it for a time doubtful whether he would not become a royal ward, but the case went at last in favour of his independence, and he found himself at eighteen the master of a small property and responsible for the care of his mother and several unmarried sisters.

Whether in these circumstances Cromwell had the leisure or resources to study law is doubtful. Tradition assigns him to Lincoln's Inn, although most of his kinsmen and friends were at Gray's. The registers of these Inns, as also of the Inner and

Middle Temple, know nothing of him. He was, however, in London for some time during his twentieth and twenty-first years, for he had an introduction to a wealthy leather-merchant, Sir James Bourchier, whom he visited at his London house on Tower Hill and at his country house in Essex. Sir James' five sons were still children, and it was not their company, but that of their elder sister, Elizabeth, which Cromwell sought. The marriage was not so brilliant on either side as to preclude the possibility of a love-match. Cromwell's approach to individuals was always impulsive and sincere; he may have found in the company of this dull and tranquil young woman an antidote to the restlessness and self-questioning of his own nature. She was twenty-three, two years his senior, and we know too little of her to speculate on her feelings. They were married in London at St. Giles' Cripplegate on 22 August 1620.

Cromwell now returned to Huntingdon with his wife. A son, Robert, was born fourteen months later, followed by Oliver in 1623, Bridget in 1624, Richard in 1626, Henry in 1628 and Elizabeth in 1629. Cromwell's income, which does not seem at this time to have been much above £300 a year, was no more than sufficient to maintain his position with a growing family to provide for. His lands were largely wheat growing and a run of low prices soon after his marriage must have struck him hard.

Meanwhile the rich uncle, Sir Oliver at Hinchinbrooke, was rich no longer. Several times he had entertained the King at great expense in hope of rewards that did not come. As a result he was compelled to sell Hinchinbrooke to the Earl of Manchester, head of the rival county family of Montagu. This decline in the fortunes of old Sir Oliver must have affected young Oliver's standing among his neighbours, but as a man of intelligence and character he none the less took an active part in local politics. In 1628 he was chosen, along with a younger son of the Montagu family, to represent Huntingdon in Parliament.

Cromwell's first experience of Parliament was interesting, even exciting, but also frustrating. It was now the fourth year of the reign of King Charles I and this was his third Parliament. He had been popular at his accession, because he had seemed eager to restore the declining prestige of England abroad by defending the Protestant interest in Europe against the Roman Catholic powers and especially Spain. Charles had indeed been ambitious for glory, and keenly interested in expanding the long neglected navy, but he was, like his father before him, entirely swayed by a personal favourite, the Duke of Buckingham. Buckingham was brave and generous – especially to his own family – and a discriminating patron of the arts, but he lacked almost every essential quality of a statesman or a leader in war. King Charles's interventions in Europe were wholly disastrous and Parliament refused subsidies while Buckingham remained in power. In 1626 the King had to dissolve Parliament to save the favourite from impeachment. By the time his third Parliament met Charles had lost all the popularity he had ever enjoyed.

This Parliament, Cromwell's first, was as critical of the King's policy as its predecessors had been. In the first session it wrenched from him his consent to the Petition of Right, a document which guaranteed the liberties of the nation and added a new one, freedom from the forcible billeting of troops, a method which Charles had recently exploited as a threat to his critics.

During the summer recess Buckingham was murdered. The King never forgot or forgave the heartless rejoicing of his people during his own bitter grief. Yet, with the great obstacle between the King and the Commons thus removed, an understanding with Parliament might have been reached. Unhappily Buckingham's death merely pushed into the forefront of affairs another cause for disagreement – the King's religious policy.

Charles believed in the reformed faith as it had been sanctioned in the reign of Queen Elizabeth, with set forms of worship according to the Book of Common Prayer and a seemly hierarchy of clergy from archbishops and bishops downwards. But an increasing number of his subjects regarded the English Reformation as incomplete, a mere compromise with Popery. They noticed with dismay the King's exclusive favour to clergy of his own opinions and the checking, discouragement or downright persecution of those who opposed them.

In the second session of Parliament the Commons attacked the King's religious policy. Cromwell's first recorded speech was a brief account of the manner in which his old friend and schoolmaster Dr. Beard had been reprimanded and threatened for venturing to criticise the 'flat popery' preached by one of the King's most favoured clerics. The speech was short but very much to the point and at least three of those present took notes on it.

The debates on religion were barren. When the Speaker, obedient to the King's will, attempted to prevent further discussion, a group of young members, chief of them Denzil Holles, pounced upon him and forcibly held him to his chair while the House passed resolutions against Episcopacy. This rude action brought King Charles' patience to an end. He dissolved Parliament by proclamation and determined henceforward to rule without it.

Cromwell's hand had not been with Denzil Holles, even if his heart had, which was as well for his family, since Holles and his confederates went to prison, pending the King's pleasure. For the next quiet years Cromwell's path and Holles' lay far apart: they were to cross again, to run for a while parallel, and at last widely to diverge.

For the next eleven years the King called no Parliament. His personal rule was benevolent by intention but was confused and corrupted in practice by administrative inefficiency and shortage of money. Among the shifts to which the King resorted to raise funds was the revival of an ancient practice by which all landowners of a certain status had to take up the honour and the duties of a knighthood on payment of a fee to the King. Those who refused to do so were fined. Either way the King profited. Cromwell was one of the many who refused and was fined £10.

Meanwhile he was involved in local politics. A group of Huntingdon citizens had petitioned the King for a new charter soon after the dissolution of Parliament. By this, administration was to be confined to twelve aldermen and a recorder who would hold office for life. The mayor was to be chosen from among the aldermen, but the name of the first mayor under the new dispensation was written into the charter. This petition came from a group in the town who were favourable to the Court; they may well have acted on Court inspiration. Soon after they had thus established themselves in power the voices of Cromwell and others were raised against them in what the new mayor and his friends called 'disgraceful and unseemly speeches'. Among other things Cromwell and his friends accused the new administration of restricting the right of the inhabitants to make use of common land. Summoned to answer for his conduct before the Privy Council, Cromwell was persuaded to withdraw what he had spoken in 'heat and passion' and to be officially reconciled to the mayor.

Not long after he moved away from Huntingdon. In May 1631 he sold his land for the modest sum of £1,800. To this period belongs the story of his intended emigration to America; like the tales of his wild youth, it is indifferently substantiated, yet it may have some basis in fact. All the same, in spite of the apparent triumph of the King's episcopalian views and of Doctor Laud's 'flat popery', Cromwell managed in the end to square his conscience with the idea of remaining in his native land. It was not to New England, but merely to some grazing land at St. Ives that he at length removed.

With this removal his fortunes reached their lowest ebb. He

now no longer owned his land, but rented a farm, a distinction which in the seventeenth century, with its rigid social conventions, meant much. His fall in society and his stay at St. Ives were alike short. In 1636 his maternal uncle, Sir Thomas Steward, made him his heir, and soon after he moved to Ely, to take possession at last of a considerable estate and a comfortable income. Very wealthy he was not, but after the struggles of the last years his position was at last secure.

With a family which now consisted of his wife and mother, four sons and two daughters, he began his life again as a citizen of the cathedral city in the fens. Possibly his wife's health had suffered under the strain of so much house-keeping and child-bearing. A son born in 1632 had died within a few days, and not until the family had moved to Ely were the two youngest children born, the 'little wenches' of whom their father was so often to think during the campaigns of the Civil War. In February, 1637, Elizabeth Cromwell gave birth to Mary, in December, 1638, to Frances. This was her ninth and last child: she was forty years old.

Cromwell's residence at Ely witnessed his third incursion into public affairs during the King's personal rule. The occasion was the enclosing and draining of the fen country, undertaken by the Earl of Bedford and a group of 'gentlemen adventurers'. The reclamation of the land would, in the long run, increase the wealth and resources of the district. But in the meantime the profits would go to Bedford and his shareholders and the fenmen would lose the fowling and fishing rights which were a great part of their livelihood. Cromwell took up their cause and became a leading figure in the fierce local opposition to the scheme, earning for himself the nickname of 'Lord of the Fens'.

Meanwhile at Ely he was a member of what was known as the Parson's Charity for giving relief to the sick and poor. These are straws of knowledge, indeed, yet not without significance in building up a picture of an honest and independent gentleman farmer, who showed his faith in the practical work of helping the afflicted and championing the poor.

He had now reached the age of almost forty without distinguishing himself in any way. By the standards of his time, he was already well advanced in middle age. His sons, who were being educated at Felsted School, near his wife's home in Essex, were fast growing up. The eldest, Robert, was already sixteen when he succumbed to one of those mysterious and rapid fevers which decimated seventeenth-century households.

Although, long after, Cromwell was to speak of the shattering grief which this loss had been to him, he was sustained in the hour of trial by a firm faith in Providence. About a year before, in October, 1638, he had written to a friend praising the great mercies of God with a newly uplifted heart: 'He giveth springs in a dry barren wilderness where no water is. I live, you know where – in Meshec, which they say signifies *Prolonging*; in Kedar, which signifies *Blackness*; yet the Lord forsaketh me not. . . . Praise him for me; pray for me, that he who hath begun a good work would perfect it in a day of Christ.'

What torments of doubt had preceded the revelation of which Cromwell spoke in this letter must remain for ever uncertain. There is evidence that during the years at Huntingdon he had been subject to fits of melancholy. Like many Puritans, he had allowed the idea of that harsh God, in whose shadow he had grown up, to prey upon his mind.

Not merely the Presbyterian group, to which Cromwell never belonged, but all English Puritan doctrine was tinged with Calvinism. The basic tenet of this faith is the belief in predestination: a man's soul is saved neither by faith nor by works, but by grace alone. Many were the Calvinists and Presbyterians, many were the more independent yet Calvinistic thinkers – of whom Cromwell was one – whose waking hours were tortured by the doubt of their own salvation. It was therefore no simple discovery of the essential goodness of God, no revelation of Christ's message, which pierced the darkness in Cromwell's soul. Rather it was the profound conviction that he was saved; as he himself put it, that his soul was 'with the congregation of the Firstborn'.

It cannot be too strongly emphasised that to the great majority of Cromwell's Protestant contemporaries, in England and abroad, such a conviction was neither odd nor self-righteous. All men of the Calvinist, Presbyterian, Baptist and generally 'Puritan' sects devoutly prayed for such a conviction as this, both for themselves and their friends. Nor was there anything unusual in the belief which henceforward governed Cromwell's actions – that he was directly guided by the Divine Will. He did not, of course, regard himself as the infallible interpreter of God's wishes, but he tested his actions no longer by the criticism of other men, or by the light of his own reason, but by their effectiveness. If he did God's will, he must succeed: failure meant that the divine contact had somewhere broken down – that there had been sin. This it was which gave him his buoyant confidence when things went well, and drove him to 'wrestle with God' in an agony of prayer when things went wrong.

Human motives are never simple, and the use of divine justification for political action, so frequent in Cromwell's time, is suspect in our own. Cromwell's character is a better guide to his actions than his own often confused reasoning. A man of high principles and strong will, his gifts were for action rather than speculation. The conversion which had given him assurance of salvation had given him also the confidence to take decisions and to act on them in a larger sphere than the Isle of Ely.

By the time he was forty his character was fully formed. Such as he was in 1639 before he entered the open field of history, such in all essentials he would be nineteen years later when, as Lord Protector of Great Britain and Ireland, he died.

The essential features were all present in the farmer of Ely – the strong affections, the love of justice, the impulsive temper which moved him fast to action, and an impregnable faith that the Divine Purposes of God would be made manifest to him if he prayed and strove aright.

TWO

The Political Problem 1640-1642

HAD there been no Civil War in England Cromwell would have passed the last twenty years of his life as he had done the first forty, without emerging from local interests and politics into the national arena. War alone was to reveal the unexpected talent which carried him to greatness. His genius as a soldier was to make him the arbiter of England's destiny. Yet in 1639 Cromwell knew no more of warfare than he had learnt from perusing the newsbooks which reported the progress of contemporary wars in Europe and the deeds of such Protestant heroes as Maurice of Nassau in the Netherlands and Gustavus Adolphus of Sweden in Germany.

What caused the apparently smooth surface of England to split into those ugly fissures through which the flames crept up to devour the land? Three problems, so far unsolved by King and Parliament, were to cause the war. The first was administrative, the second economic, the third religious. The first was the problem of administration: what services was the State to give its subjects, how were they to be organised and who was to pay for them? The second was the problem of financial control: could the Crown continue to exercise political power without the money to make it effective in practice? The third was the problem of religion: was the land to be united in a single Church, and in *what* Church?

England in 1639 was ruled by a King with a lofty conception of his duty towards his people, who knew himself to be divinely appointed as the protector of their souls and bodies. Charles wished to save the poor from exploitation, to succour those in want, to reward the deserving, to maintain order and security throughout his lands. To achieve these ends, the first necessity was to retain unblemished his own authority which he believed was a sacred trust from God. But in practice his authority depended on the individual and unco-ordinated efforts of innumerable local officials – sheriffs, justices of the peace, vicars, masters of hospitals and almshouses, churchwardens, constables and beadles. The centralising organisation at his disposal consisted of two Secretaries of State and the Clerks of the Privy Seal and Signet. The Secretaries of State managed between them, indifferently, foreign and military affairs as well as English. The Clerks of the Privy Seal and Signet lived on nominal salaries, swollen by innumerable perquisites and petty exactions to a size sufficient to support them, with their wives and children. They were adept at extracting fees, and indeed thought of very little else. In these circumstances it is hardly remarkable that the central administration kept up only an intermittent and inadequate communication with the local officials on whose goodwill the execution of the King's ordinances ultimately depended.

Working with such instruments, it was astonishing that King Charles achieved anything at all. In fact, he started a very creditable postal service, pulled the Navy into shape, and even managed to get the neglected Poor Law functioning rather better than it had ever done before – better, but not well.

Had Charles attacked the problem at the roots and set about a constructive scheme for co-ordinating local government and tightening the central control, he might have created the basis for effective personal rule. But such an undertaking called for political gifts that he did not possess and for advisers of exceptional skill and insight. It also called for far greater financial resources than were at his disposal. His attempt to impose central control in civil affairs scarcely went beyond insisting

on regular reports from Justices of the Peace, and it was only
in the earliest years of his personal rule that his Council paid
much attention to these. Control was sporadic and slack.

Shortage of money continually hampered the government.
The King's advisers thought of some ingenious ways of raising
it, like the plan to compel landowners to take up knighthoods.
By another ancient statute Charles imposed heavy fines on
landowners who had taken over or culvitated land which had
once formed part of the Royal Forests. Outstanding offenders
among the nobility long cherished resentment for the trouble
and the loss which this caused them. At the other end of the
social spectrum, he enforced an ancient rule by which no
cottage might be built without four acres of land. This had
been a wise provision in days when the population was small
and static. But in the 1630s it was growing and far more
mobile. The revival of the old practice caused irritation and
distress. Another method for getting money fast was to sell,
usually to a courtier, the exclusive right to manufacture and
market some commodity in general use. Salt, soap, writing-
paper, pins and tobacco were among those so controlled, to the
increasing annoyance of merchants and consumers.

Finally the King imposed the tax of Ship-money which
became the most notorious of all. Yet it was in truth the most
justifiable and the best administered of his taxes. The money
was needed for the navy and was spent on it. But the tax was
very doubtfully legal. In time of national danger the Crown
had an undeniable right to levy money for defence without
calling Parliament. But there was no significant national
danger when Charles imposed Ship-money. Many of those who
had opposed the King in his last Parliament refused to pay the
tax on the grounds that it had been imposed without consent.
Unwisely, the King brought a test case against one of them,
Cromwell's cousin John Hampden: unwisely because he thus
provided a platform for public discussion of the tax. Worse
was to come: to re-inforce his position Charles asked the

Judges for their opinion on Ship-money. They did not give the unanimous support that he expected: a minority pronounced the tax illegal. This division among the King's judges, the 'lions under the throne' as Francis Bacon had once called them, was a grave blow to royal prestige.

A new and more insidious danger now began to menace the royal administration. The justices of the peace did not always approve the royal directives issued to them, sometimes out of prejudice or principle, but more often because carrying out the King's policy caused friction with their neighbours. After the Hampden case, sherriffs and justices found the collection of Ship-money increasingly unpopular. Thus, at the close of the King's personal rule, it was becoming difficult to find younger men among the gentry willing to fill those offices in the local administration which their fathers and grandfathers had regularly undertaken, both as an honour and a duty. The whole system showed signs of breaking down.

Religion exacerbated and deepened the growing discontent. Charles, like most European rulers of his time, regarded himself as responsible for his people's souls. To him, their souls were far more important than their bodies, an opinion fully endorsed by many of his subjects. The care of a soul, unlike that of a body, costs relatively little. Lack of money had therefore less effect on the King's efforts. Furthermore he had a centralised organisation for the care of souls directly under his hand in the Church of England. With the help of an Archbishop of Canterbury, William Laud, who was as zealous as he was himself and a great deal more energetic, Charles was able to effect more than he could in the civil government. Like-minded bishops whom he promoted, and a central core of able and educated clergy carried out his wishes. Episcopal visitations exposed the irregularities of parish priests and the crimes and heresies of their parishioners, which the Ecclesiastical courts proceeded to punish. Preachers of doctrines unwelcome to the King were silenced.

The King and the Archbishop did not by any means attain
their ideal of a people universally educated in the Anglican
faith and regularly attending divine worship as laid down for
them in the Book of Common Prayer. They had good men
on their side, but not enough of them. There were too few
clergy altogether, and far too few good clergy. The wilder and
more remote regions were hardly supplied with clergy at all,
and there were many ignorant and inefficient priests all over
the country. But at least a beginning was made to purify and
strengthen the Church, in the teeth of opposition. The opposition did not come from the remote, wild regions, without
schools or churches. It did not come from 'the dark places of
the land', the Welsh mountains, the Cumberland hills, the
wild Border. It came from the more populated and educated
regions. It came from those who were, in their own way, just
as vocal as the most eloquent of the bishops. It came from
those who believed as strongly as the King and Archbishop
Laud that men's souls were more important than their
bodies, but who differed from them as to how souls were to be
saved.

There were two kinds of opposition to the Anglican church.
First, there were those who believed – as the King did – in the
control of a single well-organised church, but rejected the
Anglican church because it was too close to Rome. They
wanted the well-regulated Calvinist orthodoxy of Geneva.
The second group believed in a wider freedom to interpret the
Scriptures, and vehemently asserted the right of the individual
to choose his own preacher, whether ordained or not, and to
make up his own congregation of like-minded men, regardless
of any higher authority or any parish boundary. The first
group were the Presbyterians; the second, the Separatists, later
to be called Independents. It was to this group that the con-
verted Cromwell belonged. Both groups were popularly called
Puritans.

Religious unrest ignited the explosion against the King

which caused the Civil War. It began in Scotland. The King attempted to impose on the Scots a Prayer Book based on the English model. This led to widespread protest, to the signing of the famous National Covenant, and finally to armed resistance. Charles, astounded, indignant and wholly unprepared, patched up a temporary peace and sent for the most ruthless of his servants, the Earl of Strafford, who had, during the last six years, imposed order on the turbulent province of Ireland. Strafford advised the King to make a bid for popularity by calling Parliament. He calculated that the traditional enmity between the English and the Scots would cause the Commons to rally to the King. He was wrong. The Parliament of April-May 1640 was favourable to the Scots and hostile to the King. Charles dissolved it after three weeks. He had gained nothing except a knowledge of his peril.

Cromwell, who represented the borough of Cambridge in this brief gathering, must have watched the march of events with anxious interest. His education and his conversion made him one of those to whom liberty of conscience was essential. The Scottish revolt was breathing life into the latent opposition of England; the future of religious freedom depended on the stand now being made across the border, and the success of that stand depended, in part at least, on the support of England.

About midsummer, 1640, the Scots invaded England. Strafford had counted on the invasion to provoke a reaction in the King's favour, but he again miscalculated. Charles' subjects would not help him. The army was mutinous, the country sullen, and the gentry refused to subscribe to the nation's defence. By August the King was forced to make a truce. The collapse of his policy drove him once again to call Parliament and by the beginning of November, 1640, Cromwell, again returned for Cambridge, was at Westminster.

The May Parliament had shown the more vigorous members of the House of Commons that the way lay open to them. The

King had failed to organise a party for himself. Decisive and immediate attack would overthrow his Ministers and put the control of future policy in the hands of the Commons. John Pym, the ablest and boldest of the Puritan group, speaking to some of his supporters at the opening of the new assembly, declared that 'they must now be of another temper than they were at the last Parliament.' To this ardent Puritan group, led by Pym, Cromwell belonged.

The House of Commons was dominated by the landed gentry. London and some of the ports were represented by merchants and there was a growing group of lawyers, but these two sections differed little in interests and outlook from the landed class. Almost all of them, whatever their profession, had a connection with the land. Merchants had bought country estates, just as land-owners had frequently invested in trade. Many of the lawyers had a stake in the land in the shape of some small property, and almost all the rest were the younger sons or near relations of land-owners influential in the districts which they represented in Parliament. Over and above all, connecting and soldering together the whole of the ruling class, were the indissoluble bonds of seventeenth-century family ties.

Cromwell was a typical member of the Parliamentary class. He was a small landowner, married to a merchant's daughter, whose family had in turn invested in land. The marriages of his own and previous generations of Cromwells gave him nine cousins in the Parliament of 1628, and no less than eighteen kinsmen in the House of Commons in 1640. Of these the most important were John Hampden, the hero of the Ship-money case, and Oliver St. John, both supporters of Pym.

Yet to Cromwell, as to many of his colleagues, the religious question dominated the political problem. The attack on Charles' policy and Ministers, the repeated and triumphant assertion of Parliament's financial control and the assault on the judicial and executive powers of the Crown which marked the opening months of the session were but preliminaries to the reform of religion.

Cromwell, a comparatively silent member of earlier Parliaments, was active from the beginning of this new gathering. On 9 November, two days after the King opened Parliament, a young member of Royalist sympathies, Philip Warwick, strolling into the House in all the consciousness of elegance, directed a disapproving eye towards the large red-faced man who was speaking. He noticed that the gentleman's linen was indifferently clean and that his suit had been made by a country tailor. Nor did he like the contents of his oration. Cromwell was speaking in favour of John Lilburne, whom the King's Court of Star Chamber had whipped and imprisoned for distributing in the streets a pamphlet against bishops. We do not know why Lilburne had turned to Cromwell to bring his case before the Commons. Thus at the very outset of his career Cromwell came into contact with this man whose ideas were later to confront him with the most dangerous challenge of his life.

Henceforward Cromwell's activities increased. Although he played no part in the impeachment of Strafford, the most important immediate concern of the Commons, he was on several committees, and on 31 December moved for the second reading of William Strode's bill for annual Parliaments. Six weeks later he had a sharp passage with the Royalist Sir John Strangways, in which he openly attacked the established Church.

In the first ten months of the new Parliament, the Commons under the dexterous leadership of John Pym progressively undermined the royal power. They compelled Charles to send Strafford to the block and they imprisoned Archbishop Laud in the Tower. They destroyed the direct judicial powers of the Crown by abolishing the prerogative courts. They compelled the King to sign a bill guaranteeing the present Parliament against dissolution, except by its own consent: the final repercussions of this measure would be felt at the most critical moments of Cromwell's career, long after the King's death.

One essential power the King still had : he still had supreme authority over the armed forces of the kingdom. It lay with him to raise troops and appoint commanders. As long as he still had this Power of the Sword it would be open to him, in time, to regain by force what he had lost by legislation. But there was no standing army and he could not raise troops unless some evident danger threatened the nation. In late October 1641 a rebellion broke out in Ulster and spread within a few weeks to all Ireland. An army would have to be raised to quell the insurgents. Pym and his supporters were resolved that the King should not control it; they feared he might turn it against them and not the Irish.

Early in November Cromwell, acting as the spokesman of Pym's supporters, put forward a motion in the House that the Commons should join with the Lords in asking that the command of all troops to be raised in the south of England should be given to the Earl of Essex, who was notoriously no friend to the Court. This was the first move – a feeler – towards a much more far-reaching demand.

During the early months of Parliament the King's supporters had been in a minority. But since the removal of the hated Strafford and Laud and the alleviation of the principal grievances, Pym's majority had dwindled. A moderate party had begun to emerge, opposed to Puritanical reforms of the Church and against any further reduction in the King's power. It was chiefly to test the strength of the King's new supporters that Pym brought before the House the massive document known as the *Grand Remonstrance*. The *Remonstrance* was a lengthy and detailed indictment of the King's policy throughout the whole course of his reign. In effect it was a vote of 'no confidence' in Charles. If it passed the Commons then Pym's road was open to press for Parliamentary control of the armed forces. If it failed to pass, then Pym had lost his majority and must think again. On 22 November 1641, in a debate that lasted beyond midnight, the *Remonstrance* was carried by eleven votes.

It was a near thing, but Pym could still press on. On 7 December one of his most prominent supporters, Sir Arthur Haslerig, put before the House the Militia Bill for making Parliament responsible for appointing the principal commanders in the armed forces of the kingdom.

Charles, who saw the basis of all his power in danger, planned a counter-attack. On 4 January 1642, supported by the royal guards, the Gentlemen Pensioners as they were called (the small force which was undoubtedly his own and no one else's), he marched down to Westminster, entered the House of Commons and demanded that Pym and his four principal supporters be delivered into his hands. They were not in the House. Forewarned a few minutes earlier, they had escaped by way of the river. Charles departed, empty-handed and crestfallen. Nothing is more absurd than a *coup d'état* which misfires. And nothing could have been more apposite for Pym. Charles had given the strongest possible evidence that he could not be trusted to respect the liberty of Parliament if he had force at his command.

From that moment peaceful settlement was impossible. Unable to defend their cause in debate at Westminister, Charles' leaderless supporters, both in Lords and Commons, abandoned London and many followed the King himself to York. All the spring and summer of 1642 the opposing parties gathered strength, King and Parliament sending out rival commissions for recruiting soldiers, and each attempting to secure the ports and fortresses of the land. Towards the end of April Charles tried to enter Hull; the governor closed the gates in the name of Parliament. This came to be seen as the first act of war, but an armed clash came only in July at Manchester, and the King did not declare war until August.

THREE

The Military Problem
1642-1644

DURING these last critical weeks Cromwell had been active. On 14 January 1642 he had proposed the appointment of a Committee to put the kingdom in a posture of defence. A little later he offered, out of his own comparatively small resources, £600 for the reduction of the Irish rebels and £500 for the defence of Parliamentary rule in England. The summer found him in his own county busy organising its defences. He seized the magazine at Cambridge and prevented the despatch of the college plate to the King. In the late summer he received his captain's commission from Parliament, while his eldest surviving son, Oliver, now nineteen years old, took up arms as a cornet.

In July Parliament had appointed the Earl of Essex commander of its army. A soldier, with some reputation acquired in the Low Countries, Essex had been prominent among the opposition to Charles in the House of Lords. He did not doubt that the King could be made to yield to the will of Parliament, but he was no republican, and of overthrowing monarchy, or even this particular King, he had no idea.

At this time Cromwell also believed in the authority of King in Parliament with the emphasis on the latter. But his politics were closely interwoven with his religious convictions and he fought not only for Parliamentary rule but for the greater freedom of conscience that he believed Parliament would establish. As for the way to this ultimate goal, Cromwell followed it from day to day, fixing his eyes on the practical steps to be taken and solving the difficulties as they arose. The first problem was the successful waging of the war.

Parliament had the great advantage of possessing the capital and had also, by timely action, gained control of the fleet. The country was much divided, but more by regional interests and rivalries than by political principles. The King was strongest in the West Midlands, Wales and the Southwest, Parliament in the Eastern and South-eastern counties. On 22 August Charles raised his standard at Nottingham but finding insufficient support retreated to the Welsh border to recruit his forces. By mid-October he was advancing across the midlands intending, by way of Oxford, to strike the London road.

In Warwickshire, Essex, with the main body of the Parliamentary army, attempted to cut him off, and in a strong position on Edgehill, overlooking the village of Kineton, the King gave battle. The engagement, bloody and indecisive, resulted, thanks to the vigour of his young cavalry leader, Prince Rupert, in a strategic gain for Charles. He took Oxford, pushed on and might have entered London had he not been checked at Turnham Green. Baffled, the Royalist forces fell back to the University city, which now became the King's headquarters.

Cromwell had been present at the latter part of the Battle of Edgehill, although he had not taken part in the deadliest of the fighting. He had used his brain as well as his sword, noticing how Rupert's charge went through the unstable ranks of the opposing cavalry, and seeking to find the reason and the remedy. Going straight to the root of the matter, he spoke his mind to John Hampden. 'Your troops,' he said, 'are most of them old decayed serving-men and tapsters and such kind of fellows: and . . . their troops are gentlemen's sons, younger sons and persons of quality . . . you must get men of a spirit that is likely to go on as far as gentlemen will go: or else you will be beaten still.' John Hampden's agreement to this statement, even according to Cromwell's account of the interview, was of that perfunctory kind which is commonly given to persons who state obvious but irremediable truths.

Cromwell was not the man to abandon the idea merely because its realisation seemed impossible. He set himself, if not absolutely to remedy the type of recruit, at least to evolve some method by which the material ready to hand could be made serviceable.

The significance of the theories which he now evolved becomes greater when they are considered in the light of contemporary military practice. The professional soldiers who, after years of fighting in European wars, now returned to take commands under King or Parliament had to adapt themselves to conditions very different from those to which they were accustomed. The long continuance of war in Europe, and especially in Germany, had demoralised the armies. Lack of pay compelled the troops to live not merely by casual plunder, but by organised banditry. Although the higher ranking officers usually, but not always, had scruples about changing sides, private soldiers who surrendered commonly enlisted in the victorious army. As for the civilian population, whatever their allegiance or religion, they had everything to fear and nothing to hope for from any of the armies.

In England conditions were different. In the first place, prisoners had to be provided for, since the troops did not, in the early years at least, change sides with the automatic ease common abroad. The extreme inadequacy of the arrangements made for prisoners is in itself eloquent of the inexperience of even veteran commanders in dealing with such a problem. Besides, in England the civilian, for whose alleged rights the war was being fought, was more important than in any European country. The people had to be conciliated, not quelled, and Prince Rupert, who began by demanding blood-money from the town of Leicester in the fashion universally approved and practised by every commander in the German wars, was firmly ordered by the King to give it back. The management of the troops on both sides was marked by consideration for the needs of civilians; the discipline of Prince Rupert's cavalry for instance, in spite of the charges brought against it, compares favourably with that of most commanders in the later stages of the German war.

Yet professional mercenary armies had one advantage over troops raised locally in the English war. They were more mobile. Many of the English recruits believed that their duty was to defend their own county; they would not willingly march far from home or join forces with men from other regions. In the first winter of the war, in order to achieve some kind of unity among the troops from East Anglia, the Eastern Association was formed under the chief command of the Earl of Manchester. Thus something like a solid Parliamentary bloc came into being with headquarters at Cambridge. Meanwhile Cromwell, who by active recruiting and training had expanded his original troop of horse into a regiment, was raised to the rank of Colonel and made his mark as an outstandingly able and energetic officer.

In the first flush of enthusiasm, the Commons offered to provide not only pay but equipment for the recruited men, an arrangement which doubtless much assisted Cromwell in his early struggles. But very soon money gave out. By April, 1643, he was already lamenting that he had exhausted his private means, was in sore need of pay for his men and could get nothing from Westminster. Unlike the professional commanders, he was far from accepting the position as inevitable. He had raised his troops on a system of his own and was determined that they should be honourably treated. 'If you choose honest godly men to be captains,' he wrote, 'honest men will follow them.' This was an unorthodox method of recruiting, but Cromwell stood by it. His intention was to have men individually and corporately conscious of the cause for which they fought, so that their dogged resolution would match the fire of their opponents. By asking and expecting the impossible, he almost got it. Noticeably there were few foreign-trained officers among his own troops. His captains, like himself, were amateurs, learning by immediate experience, and were chosen for character and ability regardless of their social position. This method, at variance with the usual practice of the time, soon caused annoyance to some of his noble colleagues.

Cromwell's letters are more full of the honesty and godliness of his troops than of their military skill, but he had not neglected this side of their training. His careful drilling and instruction bore early fruit. At the end of April, after disarming the Huntingdonshire Royalists, he re-took Crowland; on 13 May he defeated a superior number of Royalist cavalry near Grantham and before the end of the month had pushed forward into Nottinghamshire. He was now ready to join forces with Lord Fairfax and his son in the divided county of Yorkshire, where they were struggling to establish the ascendancy of Parliament.

Treachery brought the plan to nothing. The Governor of Hull, that same Sir John Hotham whose defiance of the King had initiated the war, was now in correspondence with the Royalists. The vigilant Cromwell discovered his plotting and helped in the denunciation and arrest which brought Hotham and his eldest son to their death on Tower Hill. But for the time being the northern advance had to be abandoned.

In the late summer and early autumn the troops of the Eastern Association renewed the campaign. Cromwell with Manchester and Lord Willoughby advanced through Lincolnshire, while the younger Fairfax and some of his troops joined them from the north. On 28 July 1643, Cromwell took Gainsborough, and on 13 October inflicted a defeat on the cavalry of the Lincolnshire Royalists at Winceby. At this engagement, during which his horse was killed under him, Cromwell first decisively proved the new spirit of his men. Their fame began to spread rapidly in the enemy ranks.

In the meantime Manchester had been named commander-in-chief for the Eastern Counties, with Cromwell as one of his four assistant colonels. He was in fact, if not in name, the second-in-command and in October he was given the responsible post of the governorship of the Isle of Ely. Cromwell was too able a subordinate to be easy to work with, and his disapproval of the ineffective Lord Willoughby culminated in a complaint to the House of Commons which led to Willoughby's resignation. Up to this time he appears to have agreed fairly well with Manchester: several months were to pass before he was to try the same methods with more far-reaching effect on his chief commander.

Cromwell did not forget his ideals in the business of fighting for them. He strenuously kept up the standard of godliness among his troops and used his first important appointment to further the cause of the Puritans. As Governor of the Isle of Ely, he not only gave free licence to new sects, but within a short while suppressed the Anglican service in the Cathedral. Marching into the lofty building one January day in 1644, he summoned the officiating clergyman to quit the building. The priest, bold in his own way and not to be put out of countenance by one of his own parishioners, continued to intone. 'Leave off your fooling and come down, sir,' shouted Cromwell. And with that made an end of singing in Ely Cathedral for the next sixteen years.

It was shortly after this that his soldier son, young Oliver, died suddenly of a fever at Newport Pagnell, where he was with the garrison. Cromwell's eldest child was now the earnest and devout Bridget, whose soul storms found their way even into the pages of her father's letters. The eldest surviving son was the incorrigibly indolent and good-natured Dick.

Political events usurped the time which might have been spent in grieving. The winter of 1643-4 brought a change in Parliamentary policy which was to be decisive. Pym had died at the end of December, leaving as his legacy to the Parliamentary cause a newly-signed treaty with the Scots. Their alliance had been essential to turn the fortunes of war. The arms and men which they were in a position to give would weight the scale in Parliament's favour, particularly in the divided north where the Royalists would now have to fight on two fronts. Feeling immediate help to be more important than ultimate concessions, Pym had bought Scottish friendship by agreeing that the English Parliament should subscribe to the Solemn League and Covenant and impose the Presbyterian religion on England when the war was won.

Although he died before the final completion of this obligation, Pym had rightly calculated the feelings of his fellow Parliamentarians. Even those who were not in sympathy with the rigid organisation of the Presbyterian Church felt that Scottish help could not be too dearly bought. Some, like Cromwell, postponed taking the Covenant for as long as possible, but did so in the end. As a true believer in liberty of conscience, he could not whole-heartedly accept the teaching of Calvin and Knox. But the time had not yet come for argument : that could wait until the King was defeated.

Yet both in Parliament and army a fissure was already there, beneath the surface, ready to split the King's opponents into hostile factions as soon as the pressure of war should be removed. On one side was the Presbyterian group, who wished the terms of the Scottish treaty to be put in force. Chief among them was Denzil Holles. On the other side were those who, like Cromwell, had been ready to bargain for Scottish help, but were resolved in some way or other to have toleration for 'tender consciences' when the religious question was finally settled. From the signing of the Scottish treaty the party later to be so widely and fearfully known as the 'Independents' had come into being, and Pym, bequeathing a strong coalition for war to the Parliamentary cause, bequeathed also the schism which was to make the war of no avail.

FOUR

The Military Problem Solved
1644-1646

In February, 1644, immediately after the signing of the Scottish treaty, a Committee of Defence for Both Kingdoms was set up, to which Cromwell was appointed. Early in January the Scottish army under Lord Leven and David Leslie, veterans of the German wars, crossed the Cheviots, deep in snow. Cromwell, who had passed the earlier part of the year stamping out abortive Royalist movements in Buckinghamshire, joined Fairfax in May at the siege of Lincoln and proceeded thence across the Yorkshire border to join with the Scots in the siege of York.

The Royalists defended the city with great valour, knowing that a strong relieving force under Prince Rupert was on its way from the south. During the intermission of warfare the Parliamentary generals received Sir Harry Vane at their quarters before York. Since the death of Pym, Vane was felt by many to be the most dynamic figure in the Commons. More of a theorist than Pym, Vane was already beginning to express Republican views, and he had come to make an exploratory suggestion for the deposition of the King. All three generals, Fairfax, Manchester and Leven, rejected the idea outright.

Cromwell's opinion is unknown, but a coolness with Manchester seems to have started at about this time. Nevertheless, tension with Manchester cannot be taken as definite proof that Cromwell had differed from his superiors in this matter of Vane's plan. He was always suspicious of Parliament's noble and wealthy supporters and he was at this time friendly with Vane. His own officers were often artisans and small tradespeople, and he had hounded Lord Willoughby mercilessly out of his command because he did not think that he was fit to discharge it. But if Cromwell was not at this time, nor for some time to come, a republican, yet he regarded Charles' deposition as a solution not to be left wholly out of account.

For the time being, military events forced political disputes into the background. Prince Rupert, a strategist of acknowledged distinction, who had meanwhile organised the King's cavalry into a flexible and deadly weapon, skilfully outmanoeuvred the besiegers and raised the siege of York. Then harassed by news of the King's difficulties in the south, he decided to engage the enemy, if he could, in a pitched battle and to put their army out of action for good. About seven miles to the south-west of York, on Marston Moor, the two armies faced each other, Prince Rupert taking up his ground with his cavalry about nine in the morning on 3 July, and the infantry under Newcastle joining the main body of the army all too slowly during the course of the day. The Parliamentary army under Fairfax was at first outnumbered because the Scots, on a report that Rupert was making for Tadcaster, had gone in pursuit. But in response to messages from Fairfax they rejoined him in the course of the afternoon.

Had Newcastle's infantry reached the Moor earlier in the day, Rupert could have fought with the advantage of numbers. By the time Newcastle came, Leven also had returned and the advantage was with Parliament. The Prince drew up his own cavalry fronting the muddy lane which straggled across the moor between the two armies and having in front of them a deep ditch. It was clear from this arrangement that the Prince did not intend to initiate the conflict. Should the opposing forces attack – he knew that he had Cromwell to face and was on his mettle – he meant to act on the defensive, with the help of the ditch which should break the force of the enemy's charge. Far out on the right flank he had placed a reserve of cavalry which was to close in on Cromwell when his troops were fully engaged in front.

The day was damp and heavy, and towards six in the evening, although the sun was not to set for three hours yet, the light was so uncertain that, to Rupert's professional judgment, there could be no action that night. The Royalist lines broke up for supper.

Cromwell, who had no professional inhibitions about starting a battle at a late hour, waited for no orders, but instantly charged.

Even then the Prince might have made good his defensive tactics had not his reserve on the flank, instead of waiting until Cromwell was fully engaged, intervened before the two forces had closed and fatally hampered their own side. Rupert rallied his men, and for about half an hour it seemed uncertain which way the conflict would go. But then, wave upon wave, came Leslie's Scots breaking against Rupert's now undefended flank. Outnumbered, without a reserve on which to fall back, the Royalist cavalry began to break and scatter. By seven o'clock they were in full flight.

Victorious on his own side of the field, Cromwell now turned to see how the fight went elsewhere. On the far side Fairfax had been driven back by George Goring, but Goring's cavalry, thinking all was well with their friends, were pursuing the defeated troops and showed no sign of coming back before night-fall. In the centre the Royalist infantry held the opposing forces in check, locked in a struggle of which the issue was still uncertain. All therefore depended on the use made of his victory by Cromwell, Leslie and the cavalry on the Parliamentary left. It was then that Cromwell executed that brilliant and dangerous move which won the battle for Parliament. Turning his troops and re-forming them in the now failing light, he swept across the middle of the field between the Royalist infantry and the reserve and took up his stand on the farther side of the field in the position held by Goring at the beginning of the struggle. The King's infantry, thus surrounded on all sides, died fighting. Some of Goring's cavalry, returning too late to relieve their comrades, fell themselves into the hands of the victors, among them Sir Charles Lucas, Newcastle's cavalry general. Of the King's men, 4,000 had been killed, 1,500 taken.

'God made them as stubble to our swords' Cromwell wrote afterwards. And Rupert was the last to underestimate his victor; it was he who in the hour of defeat gave him the name which was to remain with his men, 'old Ironside.' Marston Moor was a turning point in the war : it lost the north for the King and it established the reputation of Cromwell's cavalry.

His young nephew had been killed in the battle, and two days later from the camp before York he was writing to his sister's husband, Valentine Walton: 'Sir, God hath taken away your eldest son by a cannon-shot. It brake his leg. We were necessitated to have it cut off, whereof he died. Sir, you know my trials this way. . . . .' It is the only reference in all his letters to the death of young Oliver.

The King was not yet defeated. On the contrary, he had won victories in the South which seemed almost to offset his disaster in the North. He had defeated Parliament's General Waller at Cropredy Bridge, and only a few weeks after Marston Moor he trapped the Earl of Essex at Lostwithiel and compelled him to escape by sea, deserting all his infantry.

With the war going so badly in the South, divisions and discontent broke out between Cromwell and Manchester in the North. Manchester failed to follow up the Royalist defeat, was irritable when pressed to do so, and refused utterly to hasten his forces to the rescue of the discomfited Commanders in the Midlands and the West. Cromwell became restive, then frankly insubordinate. He accused Manchester and his lieutenant General, the Scots professional Crawford, in the House of Commons. It was a peculiar situation, for as a member of

Parliament he had a right to criticise his superior officers in a way which was clearly disloyal in a soldier.

The situation at Westminster was by this time heavy with suspicion. The Scots had not ceased to press for the reform of the English church on the Presbyterian model. A group of their most eminent divines was in consultation with the English ministers to work out a settlement acceptable to both parties. But the part that Cromwell's men had played in the victory at Marston Moor had given a new prestige to the sectaries. The Independents, as they were now called, had appeared as rivals to the Scots in their service to Parliament's cause, and it was evident that they would want some reward in the form of liberty of conscience.

Cromwell was in his seat in the Commons during part of September. His attack on Manchester enraged the House of Lords and his attack on Crawford enraged the Scots. But with a tactical skill which he must surely have learnt in the field rather than in Parliament, he now withdrew his pressure from both these men and applied it unexpectedly elsewhere. He agreed to withdraw his accusations on the understanding that Manchester would immediately march to intercept the victorious forces of the King now advancing from the West. In the lull created by this reconciliation with Manchester he inspired a motion in the House of Commons for a Committee to consider the toleration of 'tender consciences' within the Presbyterian system.

Thus Cromwell and his supporters in the Commons established a bridgehead for the sectaries despite the Scots. Events in the field would soon give Cromwell another opportunity to consolidate the Independent position in the Army. Manchester moved slothfully to intercept the King and when their forces met near Newbury at the end of October, an ill-managed battle achieved no results. It was not precisely a defeat for either side, but with better co-ordination and energy the Parliamentary army could have gained a decisive victory. At a council of war Manchester now openly admitted that he did not desire to defeat the King: 'If we beat the King 99 times, yet he is King still, but if the King beat us once, we shall all be hanged.' To this Cromwell replied 'My Lord if this be so, why did we take up arms at first? This is against fighting ever hereafter. If so, let us make peace, be it never so base.'

The inevitable outcome was a new attack by Cromwell on Manchester in the House of Commons. Once again the Lords and the Scots came to his defence, and once again Cromwell – probably assisted by that astute parliamentary strategist Harry Vane – withdrew pressure in one sector and made a surprise attack in another quarter. He declared that in time of crisis quarrels between commanders should be shelved, in the interest of a more efficient prosecution of the war. He was undoubtedly behind the measure now put forward in the Commons. This measure, which came to be called the Self-Denying Ordinance, prohibited members of either House of Parliament from holding commissions in the Army. On the face of it this was a sensible way to prevent the disruption of military affairs by political quarrels, and Presbyterian sympathisers failed to see its real meaning until too late. Its first effect was to remove all peers from their Army commands. Manchester and Essex had no alternative but to resign. At that time no mechanism existed for opting out of a peerage. But it was open to any member of the Commons who wished to stay in the Army to resign his seat in Parliament. Even this however proved unnecessary as the Commons took it upon themselves to make exemptions to the ordinance when it suited them.

During the winter the Army was further reorganised, into what they hopefully called a New Model. Regional groups were at last brought together under a single commander in chief, the best professional soldier in England, Sir Thomas Fairfax. And Fairfax without prompting asked for Cromwell as Lieutenant General of the Horse; he knew he could not do without him. The Commons gave the necessary exemption.

Meanwhile at Oxford Rupert, now in command of all the King's armies, was preparing the campaign for the coming summer. The campaign opened in mid-May with an offensive across the Midlands culminating in the capture of Leicester on 31 May. Fairfax marched to intercept the Royalists sending at the same time to Cromwell to join him with all speed. Cromwell and the Ironsides reached Fairfax's headquarters a few miles from Market Harborough on the night of 13 June 1645.

Since the taking of Leicester the Cavaliers were in good spirits and the more sanguine members of the King's Council of War believed that they could not fail to defeat Fairfax and his 'New Noddle Army' as they contemptuously called it. They had therefore manoeuvred for a battle. Even before Cromwell joined him, Fairfax had the greater numbers. With Cromwell's troops added, the King's army was outnumbered by two to one. By then it was too late to withdraw. The battle which took place on 14 June near the village of Naseby is a landmark in the constitutional history of England, but from the military point of view it was uninteresting. It did not need Cromwell's genius to win a battle at those odds, and even the collapse of the Parliamentary left wing, commanded by Ireton, under the impact of Rupert's first charge, did no more than sway the issue for a few moments. Cromwell, who had only the insufficient and half-mutinous forces of Sir Marmaduke Langdale to deal with on his side of the battle, must inevitably have driven him off the field, even if the Royalist infantry in the centre, confused by a mistaken order, had not thrown the whole of the King's army into disarray. The rout was complete, the casualties were heavy and the barbarities committed by some of Cromwell's men on the women of the vanquished, though he was not himself responsible, are a stain on his memory and a blot on the otherwise glorious name of the Ironsides.

That evening Cromwell wrote an account of the battle to

the Speaker of the House of Commons. He concluded with a plea, or was it a warning? 'Honest men served you bravely in the action. Sir, they are trusty; I beseech you in the name of God not to discourage them. He that ventures his life for the liberty of his country, I wish he trust God for the liberty of his conscience, and you for the liberty he fights for.'

Naseby settled the outcome of the war although the Royalists desperately fought on. Cromwell and Fairfax overran the West. Bridgewater, Sherborne, Bristol, Winchester, and Basing House fell before the winter came. In the early spring of 1646 what was left of the King's western army surrendered at Truro. In April reinforcements bound for Oxford were surrounded at Stowe-on-the-Wold. Cut off on all sides Oxford still held out. The King escaped in disguise and gave himself up to the Scots. The University city at long last capitulated a year after the catastrophe at Naseby. In the last days before the surrender, Cromwell's eldest daughter Bridget joined her father in his quarters outside the besieged city and was married by Fairfax's chaplain (the pious Independent William Dell) to her father's comrade in arms, Henry Ireton. A few months earlier Cromwell had arranged a marriage for his second and favourite daughter, the frivolous Elizabeth, to an amiable Northamptonshire squire, John Claypole. But he had not been able to leave his post to attend the wedding.

The first Civil War was now over. If Cromwell had not himself won it, it could not have been won without him.

FIVE

Army, King and Parliament
1646-1649

THE twenty-two months which divided the surrender of Oxford from the outbreak of the second Civil War were a crucial period in Cromwell's career. On the interpretation of his actions at this time depends the interpretation of his whole character.

Cromwell's abilities have been variously estimated. His military success was perhaps too much dependent on special circumstances to place him among the greatest soldiers of the world, although his tenacity and his imaginative handling of tactical and psychological problems would have distinguished him in any place or epoch. Simultaneously with his development as a soldier he had become an increasingly skilful and experienced operator in Parliament.

During the next months his judgment, in an exceptionally troubled situation, was often at fault. He gravely mistook the character of the King and the temper of the Army; yet he was able at each crisis to revise his views and to change direction with a resolution which established him unquestionably as the only man capable of hewing a way out of the labyrinth. His actions will always be the subject of controversy, but there can be no serious doubt of his sincerity or of his continuing belief that he served the will of God and the welfare of the nation. Such of his letters and speeches as have survived from this period reveal his profound concern for a right, a reasonable and a Christian solution.

Oxford surrendered eight years after Cromwell's conversion; he had guided his conduct through the wars always by that conviction of God's will working within him, which he then acquired. His men went into battle singing religious songs, and each soldier carried with him a little pocket edition of the Psalms, done into English verse, which Pym's half-brother had compiled and which is used to this day in Scotland. It had served Cromwell's turn to imbue his troops with this practical religious feeling, to choose godly captains, to appoint eloquent chaplains and to impress upon his men that they were indeed fighting the battles of the Lord. But it served his turn so well only because he himself believed in what he preached. Louder and more confident grew Cromwell's trumpet-call of faith, resounding through his letters. 'With this handful it pleased God to cast the scale,' he had written after the fight at Grantham in 1643. At Marston Moor came the triumphant 'God made them as stubble to our swords'. At Naseby a wondering, almost awe-stricken joy in his victory: 'This is none other but the hand of God.'

By the end of the war Cromwell's religious confidence had greatly increased. 'I advised you formerly to bear with men of different minds from yourself,' he had written once angrily to Crawford – advice which he frequently gave to others, but rarely followed himself. He was patient only with opinions which could be reconciled with his own, and he met direct opposition by instantly and sincerely invoking the Almighty. Cromwell's understanding was good and he had not the bitter fanaticism of many of his party. But his sympathies, broad-based as they were, were incapable of intellectual enlargement, and points of view which had been beyond his compass in 1638 were beyond his compass to the end of his life. He grew in practical experience, in knowledge of men and in self-confidence; but he had come into the open field too late to change the habits of half a lifetime. When he laid down his burden at fifty-nine, he was a sadder, a wearier, a more experienced man than when he took it up at forty-one: but he was not more understanding.

The end of the war left a political situation of baffling complexity. No peace terms had yet been settled with the King. At Westminster the Presbyterians were the majority and had already begun to impose their discipline on the national Church. About two thousand Anglican clergy had been expelled from their livings, causing an upheaval in the countryside which added to the general unrest.

Discontent spread in the Army, where the proceedings of the Presbyterian majority in Parliament augured ill for the freedom of conscience for which many of the soldiers believed they had been fighting. A rich pamphlet literature had grown up in the war; pamphlets, sermons and discussions spread new ideas among the troops in the enforced idleness of peace. They were most of them very young; they had been encouraged by their chaplains and some of their officers to think about and discuss the aims of the war. Some of their preachers had enlarged on the political implications of Christian doctrine. Are not all men equal in the sight of the Lord?

John Lilburne, whose case Cromwell had taken up when he had been persecuted by the King, had since then served bravely as a soldier in the first years of the war. More recently he had been in trouble with Parliament for his vigorous defence of the rights of common men. He attacked the arbitrary powers of imprisonment used by Parliament against its critics, the privileges of city companies, the system of imprisonment for debt and the narrow franchise on which the House of Commons was elected. A ready speaker and a man of indomitable courage, he had become a hero to the London populace and to many of the troops.

The religious spirit of Independency and the political ideas of John Lilburne permeated the Army. The Army had won the war for Parliament; but now it seemed to threaten Parliament itself.

Thomas Fairfax was still commander in chief. He was a distinguished professional soldier of Protestant rather than Puritan opinions, who felt deeply his responsibility towards his men but had no understanding of the revolutionary political situation in which he now found himself involved. Cromwell was thus inevitably the dominating figure. At his side his son-in-law Ireton was emerging as a strong personality, with a skill in argument which gave him a considerable influence over Fairfax who seems to have looked to him for guidance in the unfamiliar political field.

As the situation developed it became apparent that the Independents in the Army were further subdivided into two main groups; there were the purely religious Independents, like Cromwell and Ireton, who were uninterested in the social application of their moral theories, and there were those who applied their beliefs to other spheres and demanded the radical re-organisation of society. Later to be known as the Levellers, they derived their chief inspiration from John Lilburne. It is superfluous to labour the point that the first group comprised, on the whole, men of substance, while the second was recruited chiefly from the ranks and from men of the people. The Cromwell-Ireton group, fundamentally conservative, believed in Parliament as at present constituted and a reformed monarchy. But the Levellers were beginning to press for a radically changed Parliament and the deposition of the King.

In spite of Cromwell's Independent views, the Commons had speedily rewarded him for his services. When offering terms of peace to the King before Oxford fell, they had asked for an estate for him to the annual value of £2,500 and a barony. In February, 1646, they settled such an estate on him themselves, out of the lands of the Marquis of Worcester. Yet the illfeeling against Cromwell in the Presbyterian group grew stronger. The Scots even hinted that he had given Oxford understanding with the King.

unduly lenient terms because he wanted to reach a private

Meanwhile the Commons were changing in character, with the election of new members to fill the place of those who had died during the war – or been expelled for holding Royalist opinions. The elections which took place in 1645-6 brought in many Army officers of Independent views – Harrison, Ireton, Ludlow, Fleetwood, to name only a few. But there were also some important additions to the ranks of the Presbyterians. The balance remained much the same as before, but on the whole the stronger accession of personalities was on the Independent side.

The relations of Army and Parliament centred on two problems. In the first place, would the Commons be able to raise the money necessary to disband an army long unpaid? In the second place, would they carry out the promises made in September, 1644, when toleration had been guaranteed to sectaries outside the Presbyterian Church?

Now that the fighting was over, Cromwell sought only two things – the liberty of conscience for which the war had been fought and decent treatment for the soldiers who had fought it. Four years of experience with harassed Commons and callous professionals had not made him go back on the words he had written in 1643: 'I have a lovely company . . . they expect to be used as men.' So far he was staunch in his loyalty to Parliament. 'I can speak this for my soldiers,' he had written early in 1645, 'that they look not upon me but upon you: and for you they will fight, and live and die in your cause.' He believed this to be true when he wrote it and for long after. Only by degrees did he become convinced of what Parliament already suspected – that the troops did not trust in the Commons and were not loyal.

Parliament, lacking both the money to disband the troops and the intention of tolerating dangerous opinions which had grown up in the ranks, handled the situation disingenuously and badly. At the New Year of 1647 the Scots handed over the King to their keeping. With this royal prisoner, with the legislature and the executive still in their hands, they had almost all the cards, but they were unwisely led. Holles, now the leading figure in the Commons, came of a wealthy family long concerned in politics. He was stubborn and brave, but arrogant and unable to believe that upstarts and sectaries would be able to overthrow men of established position like himself. He adopted an attitude of hectoring contempt and frankly threatened to disband the bulk of the Army, with its arrears still unpaid. A few regiments would be kept in being and these would be sent to Ireland to face the desperate task of putting down the rebellion which had now lasted for six years and brought English rule virtually to a standstill.

'God,' wrote Cromwell, 'is in Heaven and He doth what pleaseth Him : His and only His counsel shall stand, whatever the designs of men and the fury of the people be.' He had need to appeal to Heaven for the situation was fast passing out of his control. Over-confident of his own powers, he had tried during the spring of 1647 to use his personal influence to secure an accomodation between Army and Parliament. He sincerely feared the consequences of rebellion on the part of the Army against the highest constitutional authority in the land – the two Houses at Westminster. But he was human, and he may as sincerely have seen the way to acquiring extra-ordinary powers and prestige by constituting himself the architect of the new peace. Ambition, however little he himself recognised it, can hardly have been absent from his plan, although it was certainly not the dominating consideration. His whole political outlook prompted him in the direction of settlement between Parliament and the troops.

He misjudged both Parliament and the Army. Both sides immediately suspected his good faith. Lilburne, in a pamphlet called *Jonah's Cry*, openly accused him of betraying the Army's cause and the people's liberty by his mild attitude in Parliament. The Commons, on the other hand, were determined to be rid of him as a dangerous sectary, and brought in a measure to prevent any but Presbyterians from holding commissions.

Suspected by both sides and seeing no way out, Cromwell for a brief moment contemplated taking service abroad. Events bore him onwards before he could escape. The spokesmen of eight regiments – "agitators" as they were called – appealed to Fairfax and Cromwell to lay their cause before Parliament. Growing frightened, the Commons empowered the generals to discuss the Army's grievances with the troops. The concession came too late, for the hopes of the extremists rose as Parliament showed signs of weakening. On May 20 1647, Cromwell reported to the House that he thought the troops would disband, but it was useless to think of sending them to Ireland. The Commons thanked him for his services in the usual polite formula. But they were not feeling polite. By this time they were frightened, and as frightened of Cromwell as of anyone else. They fancied that he knew a great deal more about the unrest in the Army than he admitted.

His actions during the next fortnight bore out their worst suspicions, for it was at this time that he made the first of his rapid changes of policy. Recognising that a dangerous deadlock had been reached between Parliament and Army, Cromwell could now only side with the Army.

Parliament continued to order disbandment, with much of the pay still owing, and service in Ireland as the only alternative. Fairfax, after a general meeting of the officers, could only inform Parliament that these orders were unacceptable and warned them that he feared 'disorder or worse inconveniencies'.

Meanwhile in London Cromwell had secretly given orders to Cornet Joyce to go at once to Holmby House where the King was held prisoner and prevent Parliament from moving him to Windsor or Westminster. He saw very clearly that if it came to open conflict between Army and Parliament, the possession of the King would be a trump card. Immediately after, on the night of June 3-4, he himself left London. Not a minute too soon : his enemies in Parliament were planning to arrest him, wrongly believing that if they did so the trouble in the Army would cease.

The tables were turned on Parliament. The King, without whom neither party yet contemplated a settlement, was brought to the Army at Newmarket by Joyce, treated very respectfully by Fairfax, Cromwell and Ireton, allowed to see some of his old servants and, in accordance with Independent views on freedom of conscience, permitted to choose his own chaplains. All these privileges had been denied him as a prisoner of Parliament. Arrangements were also made for his children to visit him. In the circumstances he seemed very willing to discuss the settlement of the Kingdom with his new captors.

Would it therefore be possible to make a settled peace in the country if the King and the Army united to impose a settlement on Parliament – a settlement which would favour the Independents at the expense of the Presbyterians and would, in some degree at least, reform the character of Parliament and curtail the power of the King? This was Cromwell's hope in the summer and autumn of 1647, but he underestimated the difficulties. It would prove impossible to find terms acceptable to Cromwell and the 'gentlemen Independents' as well as to the Levellers. Even if this had been possible, the King would have rejected them. He had no intention of conceding any part of his God-given sovereignty or making terms with men whom he privately regarded as rogues and traitors. Meanwhile he treated them courteously and played for time, while he was secretly in communication with the Scots and the Irish, whose intervention, he hoped, might ultimately restore him to his own.

Soon after the King became the prisoner of the Army, a new Council was set up to guide and control its affairs. This consisted of the general officers who had sided with the soldiers in the recent troubles, and two officers and two private soldiers chosen out of each regiment. The presence of these latter gave a spurious impression of democracy to a council which was in effect governed by the leading officers – the 'Grandees' as the Levellers came to call them – with Fairfax presiding, while Cromwell and Ireton swayed most of the decisions. On 15 June the Council forwarded to Parliament the Declaration of the Army which called for the immediate expulsion of Denzil Holles and his principal supporters, and went on to request a dissolution of the present Parliament so that a new election might bring to Westminster men who were more in touch with the present needs of the nation.

A tense six weeks followed, while the House of Commons wavered, and in the Army quarters Ireton sketched out the terms of a settlement – the Heads of the Proposals – which suggested moderate constitutional reforms. These turned out to be too strong for the King and not strong enough for the Levellers. In the uncertain situation, with the Army within threatening distance, London became a prey to disorder. Holles and his supporters were now openly raising forces to defend the capital. There were violent scenes in Parliament when a mob broke in – apprentices who had been worked up in the Presbyterian interest – and terrorised the Speaker and all Independent sympathisers. Next day the Speakers of both Houses, accompanied by a flock of Independent members, rode out of London to seek the protection of the Army. Fairfax and Cromwell were already on the march; the fugitives were received with acclamation by the Army, 20,000 strong, drawn up on Hounslow Heath. Three days later, on 6 August 1647, the soldiers, laurel crowned, marched into London to shouts of 'Lords and Commons and a Free Parliament'. They reinstated the Speaker and the fugitives, while Denzil Holles and his supporters fled before them. As for the City of London, many honest citizens may well have thought that an Army, which had both discipline and purpose, might be less disturbing to trade than apprentice mobs or the ill-managed levies that the Presbyterians had tried to raise.

All the same, it was a questionable way to make Parliament free, by forcibly expelling the opponents of the Army, and by quartering troops – not indeed in the City – but within a convenient distance at Putney. The King himself was moved to honourable captivity at Hampton Court. Cromwell must have had doubts about the treatment of Parliament, necessary though he believed it to be. 'What we gain in a free way,' he was to say later, 'is better than twice so much in a forced way.'

Yet, though the presence of the Army implied force, there were mitigating factors. In expelling Holles and his party from Parliament they had expelled a group which in no way represented the serious and considered demands of the very men who had won the war for Parliament. In calling in the Army to their aid the Independent members of Parliament were no doubt appealing to force, but to force in an unusual guise. For this Army, as the soldiers themselves had said in one of their manifestoes, was not a 'mere mercenary Army, hired to serve any arbitrary power of a state, but called forth . . . to the defence of their own and the people's just rights and liberties.' The Army, drawn from many different regions and from many different trades, crafts and professions, was in effect far more representative of the people of England than any House of Commons had ever been, or was to be for many generations to come.

The immediate problem of peace was still unsolved. As Cromwell continued with his plan to win the King for a settlement in the Independent interest, he lost the confidence of the Army. His son-in-law Ireton, strong-minded, inflexible and standing much upon his dignity, had never been popular with the men. Now they heard of Mrs. Cromwell and Mrs. Ireton being received by the King at Hampton Court. This set off more rumours among the soldiers at Putney. Were these two Grandees, Cromwell and Ireton, accepting bribes from the King in the form of titles or high offices of state, to betray the cause of the honest soldiers? The Lilburnians grew in resolution and debating power, fed by a stream of pamphlets from London.

In October they confronted the Council of the Army with the first of many documents called *The Agreement of the People*. It was a well-phrased, brief and constructive statement of their immediate aims: the dissolution of the present Parliament which had sat for far too long, new elections based on a re-distribution of boroughs in accordance with the present size and distribution of the population, biennial Parliaments thereafter, freedom of conscience and equality of all before the law. In conclusion they strongly objected to any consultation with the King about the future settlement of the country. Though they did not call him a criminal or openly demand his trial or deposition, they stigmatised him as the man 'that intended our bondage and brought a civil war upon us'.

In answer to this, the 'Grandees' called a general meeting in Putney Church to discuss the document. Both sides spoke freely. Colonel Rainborough, perhaps the highest ranking officer to be in full sympathy with the Levellers, seemed to be advocating manhood suffrage: 'The poorest He that is in England hath a life to live as well as the greatest He, and therefore, truly, sir, I think it clear that every man who is to live under a government, ought first by his own consent, to put himself under that government.'

Ireton, standing out stiffly for the superior rights of property owners, declared that only those who had 'a permanent fixed interest in the kingdom' ought to have a voice in government. Cromwell used his diplomatic skill, which was considerable when he chose to exercise it, to prevent a breach and to keep the matter within the bounds of civilised debate. In the end it was decided that the various statements put out on behalf of the Army during the last months should be considered and compared together: in effect the argument was postponed.

For his own part Cromwell was out of sympathy with Rainborough's views. His religious opinions had never been of that adventurous kind which reject the social and economic order. His pre-occupation with the individual soul and freedom of conscience had never led him to believe in the social equality of all men. Souls were equal before God but incomes and responsibilities were not.

Meanwhile he spoke common sense at Putney. He admitted the merits of the *Agreement of the People*, but pointed out the dangers that arise from a too sudden application of drastic remedies. 'Truly, I think . . . we are to consider the probability of the ways and means to accomplish it . . . There will be very great mountains in the way of this . . . It is not enough to propose things that are good in the end; but it is our duty as Christians and men to consider consequences.'

The Levellers' programme was too dangerous in the present conjuncture of affairs. It would lead to confusion and anarchy. Now, as later, Cromwell was more concerned to re-establish civil government on a firm basis than to try out unfamiliar remedies. He had fought to establish Parliamentary government as he understood it, and to ensure freedom of conscience to honest Christians, but he had never contemplated any radical change in the old established order of King, Lords and Commons, still less in the structure of society.

The limitations of Cromwell's political thought prevented any practical application of the Leveller programme. He, more than any other single man, deflected the revolution. In the circumstances, this was probably fortunate; in the existing state of English society, the Leveller programme would have roused insuperable opposition and any attempt to impose it could, in the long run, have led only to more prolonged disorder and a violent reaction.

This conservative position of Cromwell's, midway between the King and the Army, had grown untenable, when Charles himself put an end to the deadlock by his attempted escape in November, 1647. He was re-captured in the Isle of Wight within three days and imprisoned at Carisbrooke.

The King's flight, while it relieved Cromwell of the impossible burden of further negotiations, placed him in an invidious position. Whatever settlement had been arranged, Cromwell, as its architect, could not have failed to gain some personal advantage. His critics in the Army continued to assert that he had been bribed with an offer of the Earldom of Essex, and a pamphlet of that autumn declared that 'these promising patriots were but sweet-mouthed courtiers.' Very shortly after, when matters turned out differently, the Royalists started the theory that the negotiations had been nothing but a blind to trap Charles, by alternate hope and fear, into making the desperate and unsuccessful attempt at escape which put an end to the discussions and virtually signed the royal death-warrant.

That Charles' flight helped Cromwell out of an impossible situation there is no doubt: but he could hardly have planned the whole elaborate network of plot and counter-plot in which the King is alleged to have been caught, he could hardly have arranged chances and time sequences so aptly unless he had been even more closely in the confidence of Heaven than he himself believed.

The first to reap advantage from Charles' flight were the Scots. Cheated by the English Army and Parliament of their just rewards for winning the war, the Scots had reopened negotiations with the King. His flight left him with no other friends to whom to turn. In December, 1647, he signed the *Engagement*, by which he called in the Presbyterian Scots to restore him to the English throne.

Meanwhile indignation in the Army was directed alike at Charles and Cromwell. Only by undertaking to redress all grievances and thoroughly to reform the Parliamentary system did Cromwell manage to bring the troops to order again. A mutiny at Ware in Robert Lilburne's regiment – he was 'noisy John's' brother – was instantly quelled by Cromwell in person. Before the end of November an uneasy calm had been restored in the Army.

By that time Cromwell's attitude to the King had hardened. He abandoned his policy of negotiating with Charles as ruthlessly as he had previously thrown over his policy of conciliating Parliament. In the immediate outstanding problem, the problem of the disposal of the King, he found himself at last in agreement with the republicans. The change was not so quickly effected as the change of the early summer had been, for here it was not merely a policy but a principle which was at stake. Cromwell always in his heart clung to monarchy, not as a sacred institution, but as a reasonable form of government. His anger was directed against a man and not a theory.

It was now clear to him, as it had long been clear to the Levellers, that no peace could be made while the King lived. At a council of officers on 11 November, when Harrison asked that the King be proceeded against to the last extremity as a 'Man of Blood' who had deliberately deceived the peace-makers, Cromwell hesitantly conceded that, 'if it be an absolute and indisputable necessity for us to do it', then it must be done. From that time onwards his conviction of the necessity of destroying the King seems to have grown.

In December the Army Council met at Windsor to compose all dissensions. True to their beliefs, the officers held a great fast day on 23 December, Cromwell and Ireton praying devoutly with the rest. To a mind adjusted to prayer, like Cromwell's, the processes of thought are eased by such solemn appeals to God. Not long after the fast day a new note of certainty rings out again in his words and letters. In the Commons he spoke of the King as 'an obstinate man whose heart God had hardened'. He told the House that the Army would stand by them only for so long as they carried out their duties to the country: should the Commons fail in this, then the Army would fend for itself.

As the outcome of this speech, the vote of *No Addresses* was passed, by which negotiations with the King were broken off. He was now close prisoner, with no other hope in the world save in the Scots army and the projected rising of the English Royalists.

At the same time Cromwell refused to enter into any definite engagement as to his future actions, in spite of pressure from the republicans within Parliament and without. Lilburne, active and indignant as ever, burst out with an accusation of treason against him. These civilian denunciations, while they provided a background of worry, did not affect the Army, which grew in unity as the danger of a second war and a Scots invasion became imminent. Cromwell, who had been absent briefly on family business in the early spring, was back at his post in April, 1648, when a new fast and prayer meeting was called at Windsor, lasting this time for three days. The officers were now all at one in condemning those 'carnal conferences' with the King, held in the previous autumn, and early in May they unanimously passed a resolution to bring the King, 'that Man of Blood', to trial as soon as the country was at peace again.

In May the storm broke, with risings in Wales, Kent, Essex and the North, followed by a Scots invasion. Hastening first to Wales, Cromwell reduced Pembroke Castle after a siege of six weeks. Hence he marched to join Lambert in Lancashire just in time to check the Scots advance. In a three days' fight in mid-August in the neighbourhood of Preston they outflanked, defeated and captured almost the entire Scottish army. Fairfax in the meantime had trapped the southern royalists at Colchester and starved them into surrender.

But the absence of the Army from the vicinity of London for the whole of the summer had given new courage to the Presbyterians. Not only was the threat of force removed from Parliament, but a great number of the more influential Independent members, including Cromwell himself, were of course absent from the House of Commons on active service. Holles and his supporters came out of hiding, took their seats in the House and secured a vote in favour of renewed negotiations with the King. Thus the victorious Army, which had vowed to bring the King to justice, found that Parliament was consulting with him at Newport in the Isle of Wight with a view to his restoration on terms.

Throughout the autumn petitions came in to Fairfax from regiment after regiment demanding justice on all delinquents, including the King – and meaning the King first and foremost. Cromwell, from his quarters in the North where he was besieging the great stronghold at Pontefract, the last Royalist garrison in the country, forwarded a petition from his forces: it was neither the first nor the last to come in, simply one of many reflecting the bitter resolution of the Army.

Fairfax had fixed his headquarters at Windsor, and had the strong-willed Ireton with him. The unfortunate and chivalrous general did not want the King to be condemned to death, but he seems to have believed that the demand for his trial was some sort of a blind to dislodge the Presbyterians from Parliament and to quieten the extremists in the Army. He therefore authorised the presentation of a Remonstrance to Parliament asking for the trial of the King. The House of Commons shelved the Remonstrance and went on treating with Charles.

The Army was becoming difficult to control, and it was probably Ireton who urged Fairfax to repeat the tactics which had been so successful against the Presbyterians eighteen months before, namely, to march on London. Before doing so Fairfax (again with Ireton at his back?) imitated Cromwell's move of two years earlier, when he had sent Cornet Joyce to seize the King. Fairfax now ordered the removal of Charles, without consent or knowledge of Parliament, from the Isle of Wight to close imprisonment in Hurst Castle on the mainland. The King was now wholly in the power of the Army.

The Army reached Westminster on 5 December. On the following two days soldiers under the command of Colonel Pride blocked the approaches to Parliament and forcibly excluded all members who had voted for treating with the King. Cromwell was on his way from the North in response to an urgent message from Fairfax, but he did not reach

London until 'Pride's Purge' was completed. He had taken no part in it and may very well have doubted the wisdom of so extreme a display of force, but he accepted the accomplished fact.

Cromwell's opinions, and even his actions, in the ensuing weeks, during which the King was brought to trial and executed, are not easy to establish. A persistent contemporary rumour credited him with a plan for restoring the King at the eleventh hour 'on his own shoulders' and so becoming the indispensible and all-powerful minister of a grateful monarch. Others believed that he even made an overture to the King for a peace favourable to the Army – an approach which the King rejected. The first story was a journalist's fabrication based on wishful thinking, and the evidence for the second is so uncertain as to be negligible.

Cromwell kept studiously in the background during most of the proceedings against the King. Eleven years later, during the trials of the surviving regicides, several of these unfortunates pleaded that he had forced and bullied them into signing the royal death-warrant. To save their own skins, they drew Cromwell in the harshest colours, but in essentials they were probably speaking the truth. He did not say much in Parliament during these weeks; he sat as one among many in the High Court which tried the King. But he used his powerful personality and, on occasion, his withering scorn to bring waverers into line. He was resolved that the King should die for his misdeeds, and had described him in telling words, when writing to allay the doubts of an old friend, as 'this man against whom God hath witnessed'. There can be no doubt that Cromwell saw the victories of the previous summer as the clear witness of God against the King.

But he was anxious that the justice of God should also be acceptable to men. Cromwell still had, and was to have until the end of his life, a deep respect for the law. He wanted the dangerous act, on which the Army was resolved, to be an act of law and not of force. He would certainly have preferred that the House of Commons, which now proceeded to set up a High Court of Justice for trying the King, should be a rather more representative assembly than the handful of fifty odd who remained after Pride's Purge. The miserable size of this Rump was not entirely due to the expulsion of the Presbyterians. A considerable number of other members had absented themselves as a protest against the use of force; among these was Harry Vane, Cromwell's old friend and associate.

We know from the brief notes of Bulstrode Whitelocke, one of the most eminent and influential lawyers in the country, that Cromwell had several meetings with him in December to see if any means could be found to bring more members back into the House before the King's trial. Cromwell also undoubtedly hoped that some of the Judges would be found willing to countenance the trial. But the two Lords Chief Justice and the Attorney General refused to act. The High Court was in the end presided over by John Bradshaw, a judge of the sherriff's Court of London who had recently been appointed a judge for the Welsh marches; the prosecution was conducted by a fanatical republican barrister from Gray's Inn, John Cook. The relative obscurity of these two men made it clear that the trial of the King was not, and could not be, countenanced by any respectable body of legal opinion.

In the circumstances it was perhaps remarkable that, of the hundred and thirty-five men appointed to sit in the Court, more than eighty appeared at one or more sessions, and fifty-nine signed the death warrant. The most notable of the absentees was Fairfax. He came to the preliminary session, and seems then for the first time to have understood that the trial was not a blind, but a trial in deadly earnest, with only one end in view – the condemnation and death of the King. From that moment Fairfax withdrew from the Court, and utterly refused to yield to the persuasions of Cromwell and Ireton that he should countenance the proceedings with his presence.

He allowed his wife – in a mask, as was usual with great ladies in public places – to attend the sessions in Westminster Hall. Masked or not, Cromwell must have known her voice when she called out from her box: 'Oliver Cromwell is a traitor.'

Fairfax himself took no further action. Years later he would say, probably with truth, that he dared make no move to save the King, because had he tried to do so he would only have divided his Army and caused instant civil war with bloodshed in the streets of London. Wretchedly bewildered and virtually powerless, there can have been few unhappier men in England than Fairfax during that cold January of 1649.

The King was brought before the Court of Justice in Westminster Hall on 20 January. With great dignity he refused to recognise their authority. He went further; he claimed that by denying the legality of the proceedings he was protecting his people from arbitrary power and the use of force. He would repeat the same argument on the scaffold and claim that he died as the people's martyr.

For three days Bradshaw tried in vain to compel the King to answer the charge made against him. He continued steadfast in his assertion that this so-called Court had no authority to try him or anyone under the laws of England. The effort to make him submit had to be abandoned, and on 27 January, although no real trial had taken place, he was brought in to hear his sentence. Even this last session did not go smoothly. The King now asked to be heard, not on trial in Westminster Hall, but in private before the Lords and Commons of his Parliament to whom, he said, he had a proposition to make. Bradshaw refused the request and was proceeding to the sentence when a member of the Court, John Downes, nervously but audibly protested. In some disorder the Court adjourned. In a stormy consultation behind the scenes Cromwell turned on Downes as a peevish troublesome fellow, and a fool as well, for being deceived by the offers of the King, 'the hardest hearted man on earth'. Leaving Downes defeated and in tears, the rest of the Commissioners filed back into Westminster Hall and sentence was duly pronounced on the King.

During the next two days those who had agreed to the sentence were called upon to sign the warrant for the King's execution. Some signed willingly, even with enthusiasm. Others hesitated, trying to evade all further responsibility. Cromwell was having no such evasions, and ruthlessly rounded up the nervous and the waverers. Of the fifty-nine signatures which were at length obtained to justify the King's death, his own name stood third.

On 30 January, 1649, Charles died, with that royal calm and Christian resignation which cast a radiance over his life and sanctified his cause in a million hearts.

The Court of Justice and its actions did not in any sense represent the people's will. Suspicious, conservative and politically uninstructed, the majority of the people believed in monarchy and were shocked at the King's death; but then as now, their private pre-occupations and their daily bread were of greater importance than the most stirring events of the political world. They were soon thinking of their future.

Cromwell was acting in the best interests of the people in so far as he realised that only through Charles' destruction could peace come to England. No compromise was possible and while Charles lived no settlement would hold. By all the canons of right and wrong as he understood them, Charles who had cheated his captors when they gave him terms, and provoked a second war, deserved death. It was plain justice, and in all his remaining life Cromwell never thought of it otherwise.

And indeed, although judicial murder is a cold and horrible thing, the King has had more than his share of pity. The Royalists naturally venerated his memory, though rather as a martyr who died for his Church than as one who died for his people. The real tragedy of the war, for which he was so largely responsible, was the thousands dead on the battlefields, shot in reprisals, deported to Barbados, starved and plagued away in prisons. The king had (like Cromwell) both courage and idealism, but he lacked the first essential for a man called on to govern : he had no imagination or sympathy for the governed. It was his misfortune that he lived to be a King. It was Cromwell's misfortune that he had to get rid of him.

Cromwell's conscience was never, so far as we know, to trouble him for Charles' blood. He had had no choice in the matter and as always he took the strong political compulsion for the voice of God. He, and many of those who stood by him in this bitter business, did indeed feel a conviction which posterity should respect, even if it cannot understand it. Eleven years later Thomas Harrison, speaking at his trial for high treason before the judges of the restored monarchy, his cause broken and his life in hazard, was to call again on that authority, higher than the King's, to which alone he owed obedience and under which he acted. 'I followed not my own judgment,' he said; 'I did what I did as out of conscience to the Lord.' He spoke for Cromwell.

SIX

Army and Parliament
1649-1654

ON 4 January the House of Commons had voted 'that the people are under God the original of all just power'. In this belief, sincerely held if strangely expressed in his actions, Cromwell had worked for the death of the King. But he was painfully aware that the small remnant now in the House could hardly claim to speak for the people, and he renewed his efforts to make the Commons slightly more representative of the nation. He accordingly secured an amendment in the declaration of loyalty that all members were now required to take, so that even those who had had qualms about the King's death could be readmitted to the deliberations of the House. This brought Harry Vane and a score of other absentees back to their seats.

The tide had now set, not only against monarchy, but against aristocracy. On 6 February the House of Lords was abolished; this was no very serious loss, for of the pitiful remnant of peers who remained the only two who were still seriously concerned in contemporary politics, Salisbury and Pembroke, immediately sought and obtained election to the Commons.

The King's death left the Army the source of all authority in England. It was an unstable power, the outcome of events, not of a constructive plan, and therefore a prey to circumstances. The crisis of the second Civil War had brought the Army together again, but as soon as the King was dead the old difficulties re-emerged. Cromwell had killed the King, but he had not abandoned his traditional attitude to law and the constitution. All this latter part of his life he was to find himself torn between his own desire for a reasonable and even a conservative settlement and the revolutionary action forced on him by the times.

Now that the King was dead the next move was to settle the government on a permanent basis. During the last weeks a group of Grandees, including Cromwell and Ireton, had held talks with some of the Levellers to work out a programme acceptable to all. Lilburne soon suspected that this was nothing but a manoeuvre to keep him quiet during the King's trial; he walked out after calling Cromwell and Ireton a pair of 'juggling knaves'. But other Levellers stayed and in due course a revised and emasculated *Agreement of the People* was put before the Commons. It did little more than recommend a dissolution of Parliament to be followed by fresh elections on a slightly altered franchise. It was at least a beginning, or could have been one, and Cromwell was in favour of proceeding with it. But Lilburne opposed it vehemently and stirred up his supporters in London and in the ranks of the Army.

The King's execution had given new life to the extreme democratic elements in the country, and in April a group of enthusiasts dug up St. George's Hill at Walton in Surrey, and planted beans, thus giving practical proof of their theory that all the land in England belonged to the people. This demonstration of the Diggers was put down in a very short time by Fairfax. Far more serious was the unrest among the Levellers in the Army, now approaching dangerously near to mutiny. Cromwell did not underestimate the danger. 'If you do not break them,' he said, 'they will break you.'

In March, Lilburne, whose pamphlets were fanning the trouble in the ranks, was placed under arrest. But it was already too late. The discontent was too widespread, the sense of injustice too strong. In May mutiny broke out at Salisbury.

The Levellers, nearly a thousand strong, marched across the Downs to Oxfordshire hoping to join with sympathisers in those parts. But they were disappointed, and when it came to a trial of arms, there was more talk than determination among them. Cromwell and Fairfax, pursuing their march and demoralising them with firm but generous appeals, soon brought over the greater number. Those that showed fight to the last were but a handful, soon destroyed. The highest officer among them, a captain, was cut down in a wood near Wellingborough making a last, desperate stand. Of the prisoners, a cornet and two corporals were shot, the two latter facing the firing party unrepentant, convinced that their cause was right. In London John Lilburne was tried, and although the jury refused to find him guilty and he was acquitted amid cheers, he knew that the failure of the Army Levellers had destroyed the strength of his party.

The forces of tradition were too strong for Cromwell to have acted otherwise than he did. Already political circumstances had carried him into waters too deep to negotiate. Now, after the King's death, as nine years before, his first thought was still for religion. He, like many others, had attacked not the monarchy but the King's Church policy. The particular quality of Charles' religious convictions had made it impossible to alter that policy without destroying him, and with him the accepted form of English government. Cromwell therefore, who had no training in political theory, no taste for it, and no desire to experiment with it, was presented by circumstances with an opportunity for making a revolution in government.

But all that he wanted in 1649, as in 1640, was security of government and liberty for tender consciences. For the revolutionary overturning of property rights, for the establishment of political equality, for the abolition of 'the ranks and orders of men, whereby England has been known for hundreds of years' he had no desire. He saw in such ideas merely causes for continual disturbance and the destruction of civil order. Lilburne accused him of betraying the cause of the people, but he had never seen their cause with Lilburne's eyes. The death of Charles I, unlike that of Louis XVI, was to those that compassed it less a bloody demonstration of the people's rights, than an obvious political necessity. Cromwell killed Charles because he thought it was the only way to bring peace to England. He shot the Levellers for the same reason.

The next important problem to be faced was the rescue of the Protestant settlers in Ireland. In the course of seven years, since the Irish Rebellion broke out in October 1641, the Irish Confederates had established an independent government at Kilkenny and had driven the settlers out of the greater part of Ireland. Involved in its own Civil War, Parliament had been unable to send help. The Lord Lieutenant, Ormonde, had remained loyal to the King, and it was only after the defeat of Charles that he resigned his command and handed over Dublin to Parliament. Since then Parliament had sent some sparse re-inforcements but had been prevented by renewed troubles in England from taking any effective action. By 1649 little remained to the Protestants except Dublin and Belfast. The Irish victory would have been complete had they not wasted their energy in vehement quarrels among themselves. The shock of the King's death brought them momentarily together. The Confederate Irish accepted Ormonde as the commander of their forces in the name of the young King Charles II, and by the summer a large Irish army was encamped before Dublin confident that the capital would soon be in their hands.

Cromwell had been appointed Lord Lieutenant of Ireland by order of the Commonwealth of England as early as March 1649. But the disturbances in England prevented him from setting out until July. He arrived in Dublin with 12,000 men, arms and supplies on 15 August to find that only a few days before the stalwart commander in Dublin, Michael Jones, had routed the Irish from their camp at Rathmines and ended the siege. The astonishing victory and the arrival of re-inforcements restored the morale of the Protestant forces, which had previously been at the lowest ebb.

Cromwell's two shattering campaigns, in the late summer and autumn of 1649 and the spring of 1650, saw the collapse of the Irish Confederation. The troops which Ormonde had at his command were scattered and ill-armed, and undermined by internal dissension. Cromwell and his lieutenants swept all before them. Drogheda fell on 11 September, Wexford on 11 October, Ross on the 19th. Sickness forced Cromwell to raise the siege of Waterford in December, but the following spring he carried his arms inland from the coast. In February he took Cashel and Cahir, in March Kilkenny, in May, after a heroic resistance, Clonmel. By the early summer of 1650 the quelling of Ireland could be safely left to his lieutenants, of whom not the least was his son Henry, at twenty-two one of the most promising young officers in his army.

The first Irish campaign is a blot on Cromwell's reputation which no specious justification can efface. At the fall of Drogheda nearly 3,000 of the defenders had been killed; at Wexford hundreds of civilians had been put to the sword. Cromwell defended himself against accusations of barbarity by asserting that he had acted according to the necessities of war, and that at all other times the discipline of his troops was good, that plunder was forbidden and that he was ready to redress any wrong done to those not actually in arms against him.

The massacre of the garrison at Drogheda was in accordance with a harsh rule of war – frequently though not invariably enforced – by which those who held out without reasonable expectation of relief could claim no mercy. But the prolonged sack of the town itself and the killing of civilians had no such military excuse. The slaughter at Wexford on the other hand was explicable if not justifiable. Wexford had been, for the last seven years, the principal base for piracy in the Irish Sea and the Channel, piracy which had cost the lives of thousands of English seamen, ruthlessly hanged or thrown overboard when their ships were captured. Hence the ferocity of Cromwell against a town which had put itself beyond the law.

So far from having misgivings about these terrible actions, Cromwell gloried in them as pleasing to God. 'The Lord is pleased still to vouchsafe us his presence and to prosper his work in our hands,' he wrote, and he spoke complacently of the 'righteous judgment of God upon these barbarous wretches'. Like most of his English contemporaries, Cromwell had read and had believed the atrocity stories printed and reprinted in England ever since the beginning of the Irish revolt. These stories were adorned – for the edification of the illiterate – with crude woodcuts showing the murder and torture of helpless English settlers. Pictures and text must have been familiar to most of the men in Cromwell's army and had built up a sense of vindictive rage against the Irish. The stories were not all baseless. The rising in Ulster in 1641 had been marked by indiscriminate sacking, burning and killing, and the fighting in Ireland ever since had been conducted on both sides (with some honourable exceptions) with great ruthlessness. The barbarities of Cromwell, a commander not usually given to such excesses, are at least comprehensible in the light of contemporary propaganda and the bitter atmosphere of the Irish war : comprehensible but not therefore excusable. They remain a dark shadow on his name.

After the fall of Clonmel, Cromwell sailed for England, where Parliament was clamouring for his help. The Presbyterian party in Scotland, in one last effort to win back what they had lost through the triumph of Independency in England, had crowned the young Charles II king and were threatening to invade England. Parliament had wanted Fairfax to march against them, but he refused on the grounds that their army had not yet crossed the border. He would be willing, he said, to take command as soon as they invaded, but he would not seek them out in their own country.

Thus in June, 1650, Cromwell was made in name what he had long been in fact, commander-in-chief of the Army. 'I have not sought these things,' he declared; 'truly I have been called unto them by the Lord.' He had in vain used all his influence to prevent Fairfax from resigning.

Cromwell crossed the Scots border at the head of about 16,000 men in June, 1650. The commander of the opposing army was that same Leslie at whose side he had fought at Marston, an experienced and cautious soldier. A month of manoeuvres failed to draw the Scots into battle and at the end of August sickness in the ranks compelled Cromwell to withdraw to the plain of Dunbar, which he intended to use as a base for future operations. Leslie saw his opportunity and, by quickly outmanoeuvring Cromwell, cut off the English between the hills and the sea. The Scots army numbered about 20,000, Cromwell's by this time not much more than half as many.

In this desperate position the God in whom he trusted once more stretched out his hand on Cromwell's behalf. Leslie, who seems to have thought that the English intended to embark on their provision ships and make the best of their way off, allowed himself to be persuaded to leave his strong position on the hills to attack Cromwell in the plain. Before the amazed eyes of the English army, the Scottish troops descended on to the flat ground. Cromwell was not likely to miss such an opportunity.

At dawn on the following day he initiated the conflict with a cavalry charge, the direction of which he left to John Lambert, while he himself conducted a movement designed to take Leslie on the flank when his front rank was already engaged. The Scots army, largely consisting of raw recruits, was no match for Cromwell's determined veterans. His cavalry proved, as always, irresistible. 'The best of the enemy's horse being broken through and through in less than an hour's dispute, their whole army being put into confusion, it became a total rout: our men having the chase and execution of them near eight miles,' he wrote that night to Speaker Lenthall. To his wife he wrote on the following day: 'The Lord hath showed us an exceeding mercy; – who can tell how great it is! My weak faith hath been upheld.' He concluded with one of his rare expressions of personal emotion: 'Thou art dearer to me than any creature.'

Cromwell did not feel towards the Presbyterian Scots as he had done towards the Catholic Irish. 'Since we came into Scotland,' he wrote to Lenthall, 'it hath been our desire and longing to avoid blood in this business: by reason that God hath a people here fearing his name though deceived.' After the Battle of Dunbar he was anxious to reach a compromise settlement, and his overtures met with a qualified success, for, although the King's supporters did not surrender, yet they were weakened by the desertion of many waverers, whose doubts of the wisdom of setting up Charles II were confirmed by the miracle at Dunbar.

Edinburgh surrendered on 19 December 1650. But Cromwell postponed the spring campaign partly because he fell seriously ill and partly to allow time for further negotiations. Not until June, 1651, did he again take the field, and this time with the definite intention of ending the war before the autumn. The question of money was, as always, acute: Cromwell knew that another winter and spring of warfare would bankrupt the Commonwealth. He therefore struck to force an immediate issue.

Pursuing Leslie northward to Perth, which surrendered on 2 August, he left the road to England open to the King and the rest of his army. Having established garrisons to hold the country and left General Monck to pacify it, Cromwell turned to follow the King's inferior forces across England. He cornered them at Worcester and here, on 3 September, the anniversary of the Battle of Dunbar, he destroyed what was left of the Royalist army. The young King and a few followers fled – after months of wandering to find refuge at last in Paris.

The last shot of the Civil Wars had been fired. Parliament voted an income of £4,000 a year to Cromwell, with Hampton Court for a country residence, and when he rode into London on his return from the campaign, accompanied by Speaker Lenthall, the streets were lined with cheering crowds. 'The generalissimo,' reported the Genoese agent to his Government, 'will do what he pleases.' The war was ended and the work of 'settling and healing' could begin.

In the eyes of the Genoese agent, and indeed of most unprejudiced observers, Cromwell was the greatest power in the country. But the Council of State and what remained of Parliament were still the theoretical source of authority. In the months during which Cromwell had been fighting Parliament's battles, Parliament had progressed very little towards settling the affairs of the nation.

There were still some able men in the Rump at Westminster, Cromwell's old friend Harry Vane among the most prominent. But there were also many timeservers, helping themselves to lucrative appointments, buying up confiscated land on the cheap: men who were abhorrent to the godly officers who returned to their seats in Parliament when the fighting was over. Cromwell, deeply respecting the idea of Parliament, was prepared to be patient with them for a time. But some of his officers, the fanatic Colonel Harrison for one, were urgent for a dissolution by force and the election of a new assembly of godly men.

Parliament had passed some useful measures in the interim and set up some committees to enquire into abuses of the law and to encourage the propagation of the Gospel. They had also, in view of the damage which had been done to English commerce during the war years by the rapid development of the Dutch carrying trade, passed a Navigation Act against the transport of English goods in foreign vessels. The commercial rivalry between the two Protestant Republics, the Dutch and the English, had reached flash point. By the summer of 1652 they were at open war.

Parliament, which had now lasted for over eleven years without a general election, made the Dutch war into another excuse for postponing their dissolution. Cromwell found the delay intolerable, but was opposed to the forcible dissolution which some of his officers wished for. He hoped for a more peaceful solution. By his own account he had been hoping, after the Battle of Worcester, to retire into private life. Others, who observed his actions, thought differently. The republican colonel Edmund Ludlow and the lawyer Whitelocke believed him to be ambitious for personal power. In a discussion of the future settlement of the country, as Whitelocke long afterwards remembered, or said that he remembered, Cromwell had declared that they could not dispense with monarchical authority, significantly asking the question: 'What if a man should take upon him to be king?'

Such a statement is not out of keeping either with Cromwell's views or with his expressed desire for retirement. The state in which he found the country after the Battle of Worcester justified him in postponing his leisure to a better time. Confident both of his own ability and of divine guidance, he was easily convinced that he had a duty to remain in office for some time longer. With his traditional political views, he may have expressed the opinions attributed to him by Ludlow and Whitelocke, rather in some exploratory groping after a solution than with any definite idea of assuming monarchical power himself.

His first constructive movement towards a settlement was to hurry an Act of Pardon and Oblivion through Parliament. While he was later to be a harsh judge of all those who sought to cause fresh disturbance in the country, he was genuinely anxious to reconcile the defeated party and to allow them as far as possible to have a share in the privileges of citizenship.

He served on several committees – on that for reform of the legal system, for laws touching the relief of the poor and for the propagation of the Gospel. On this latter committee he distinguished himself at once by advocating the widest possible basis for toleration. But work on committees meant little enough, when nothing was done to dissolve the inadequate remnant of Parliament, and to seek a new election after more than eleven years. The Army was increasingly restive. Meanwhile, the Dutch war cost money, to raise which the lands and goods of Royalists were still being confiscated. In such circumstances an Act of Oblivion, passed in February, 1652, was likely to remain a dead letter.

On 12 August, 1652, the Army officers presented a petition asking for a speedy consideration of their own and the country's grievances. They asked that steps be taken to reform the inequalities of the law; that the gospel be propagated in the remoter parts of the kingdom and that ministers be supported by some other means than tithes. They asked that places of authority should be given only to 'men of truth fearing God and hating covetousness' – this was an attack on the self-seekers in Parliament. They asked that the revenue should be reformed and accounts published. In conclusion they urgently demanded that a term be put to this Parliament and a nation wide election be held.

The Rump went so far as to appoint several committees to look into the questions the Army had raised. But over the last and most vital demand of all – the demand for a new election – they did not move so fast. There were two groups in the House – a small one consisting largely of the Army officers who wanted a dissolution, and a larger one led by Harry Vane who feared the effects of a new election and were willing only to make the present Parliament more truly representative by local elections to fill the gaps.

Cromwell exercised patience. He spoke in the House and

in Committee with studied mildness as if it had not been in his power to overthrow the Rump by a word of command. He truly respected the idea of Parliament and he still hoped for a solution which should neither be, nor seem to be, the result of force. While any hope remained that the Rump would dissolve itself, he would take no action against it.

His old friendship with Vane was visibly breaking up. This ardent Republican who, on the eve of Marston Moor, had spoken of deposing the King, had a more adventurous intellect than Cromwell but less judgment of a political situation. He misjudged it now. He was resolved to prevent a dissolution which, by removing the only recognised civil authority in the land, would make way for the rule of the Army. He did not see that the Army could no longer be resisted; power was theirs for the taking, and they would take it. He also did not see, or would not believe, that the Army had at least as good a claim to represent the people as the pitiful remnant which still called itself Parliament.

Vane was in favour of a bill to keep the Rump in being and to fill the gaps – the majority of the seats in fact – by local elections. It was suggested that this system should be adopted in future. Parliament should be in permanent session, general elections should disappear and seats should be filled up as they fell vacant.

In April 1653, to the mounting indignation of the Army, the bill was put forward. Cromwell, in discussions with Vane secured (as he thought) a promise of its postponement. But on the following day, 20 April, its supporters insisted on a debate and Vane gave way. Cromwell was absent. Colonel Harrison slipped out to fetch him. He came immediately – without stopping to change his grey worsted stockings for something less homely – but he had time to call up a guard which he posted outside the door when he took his seat. He said nothing until the Speaker put the motion 'that this bill do now pass'. Then he rose. He began by words of solemn praise for the great things done by this Parliament in its earlier heroic days, recalling the struggle against the King and all that they had done and suffered. But when he came to their present corrupted state, the stream of his eloquence thickened into a torrent of accusation. Carried forward by the flood of his own oratory, he left his place and began to stamp up and down the floor of the House, glaring and gesticulating. 'The Lord has done with you!' he thundered out at the embarrassed assembly. As he came to his climax twenty or thirty musketeers filed into the House. Cromwell shouted to the Speaker to come down. Lenthall did not move and Harrison stepped forward with a grimly courteous offer to assist him. Lenthall then gathered up his robes and made as dignified an exit as he could. The rest of the members followed him out, leaving Cromwell and the soldiers in possession of the empty room. Swinging the mace off the table, 'Take away this bauble,' he shouted. And then seeing the defeated Vane moving towards the door, burst out with vituperative scorn, 'Sir Harry Vane! Sir Harry Vane! . . . May the Lord deliver me from Sir Harry Vane!' He had already delivered himself.

The forcible expulsion of the Long Parliament made Cromwell for a brief spell the most popular man in England. A tide of hope had set in with the extinction of the despised Rump. Relief from taxation, lower food prices, justice for the poor, reform of the law were confidently expected. Within a few days of the dissolution Cromwell used his power to pardon a number of petty criminals condemned to death. He had always objected to hanging for small crimes. As he once put it: 'To hang a man for six and eightpence and I know not what, to hang for a trifle and acquit for murder . . . to see men lose their lives for petty matters, this is a thing God will reckon for.'

Meanwhile he saw himself only as the steward of the nation's affairs until a new Parliament should establish a fixed form of government. He set up a Council of State consisting of seven of his officers and three civilians. Their first work was to arrange for a Parliament to meet. But what kind of a Parliament? Now that they were themselves responsible for the decision, they saw that the free election, which had been so ardently desired, would be too dangerous in the present crisis. A provisional Parliament would have to be nominated. Harrison and his friends, who truly believed that the Rule of the Saints had come, wanted it to consist of godly men chosen by the sectarian congregations up and down the country. Realists, like Cromwell and General Lambert, wanted a wider basis of choice including men of position and experience – something more like a traditional Parliament.

A compromise was reached. The congregations submitted their lists of names, but the Council chose only some of them and added others of their own choice. Even so, the extreme sectaries were in a majority when Parliament met. Indeed it was popularly called Barebone's Parliament, from the name of Praise God Barebone, one of the members for London. It consisted of 140 members, 129 for England, 5 for Scotland and 6 for Ireland, and has therefore the distinction of being the first United Kingdom Parliament ever to meet.

At the opening ceremony on 4 July, 1653, Cromwell called upon the members in solemn language to settle the just liberties of the people in a godly Commonwealth. 'You are called with a high call,' he said, 'and why should we be afraid to say or think that this may be the door to usher in the things that God has promised?' He exhorted them also to build the state anew in a spirit of toleration. 'If the poorest Christian, the most mistaken Christian shall desire to live peaceably and quietly under you, – I say, if any shall desire but to lead a life of godliness and honesty, let him be protected.'

But the moderates in the assembly were not strong enough to stem the headlong demands of the sectaries which, however good in themselves, alarmed the City; all the more so as the more extreme sectarian ministers in London worked on their excitable congregations with vehement sermons. So far from settling an acceptable and peaceful government it looked as though the extremists at Westminster would overturn the state entirely. The crux of the matter was the abolition of tithes, urgently demanded by the sectaries and strenuously resisted by the parochial clergy and all land owners as an onslaught on property rights.

The moderates in Parliament, at this point, met by agreement very early in the morning and while they still had a majority voted the dissolution of the assembly. They resigned their power wholly into Cromwell's hands, giving him, as he himself expressed it, 'power over the three nations, without bound or limit set'.

SEVEN

Oliver Protector
1653-1655

Two Parliaments having failed to make a Constitution for England, the Council of Officers took the matter into their own hands. The document, which was short for the weightiness of its matter, was called bluntly the *Instrument of Government*. Its chief architect seems to have been General John Lambert. By its provisions executive power was vested in a Protector, controlled and assisted by a Council of State. The legislative power, on the other hand, belonged to Parliament which was to meet at least once in every three years; Acts which it had passed became law with or without the Protector's consent – always supposing they contained nothing directly contrary to the Constitution.

During the intermission of Parliaments the Protector and his Council could issue ordinances which had the force of law until Parliament met, when they had to be submitted for its final sanction or annulment. In theory at least, Cromwell thus wielded a very limited power, with no veto on legislation such as all Kings of England had possessed. The concession was perhaps more theoretical than actual for, as the Army officers well knew, the last word in any political dispute lies with those that bear the sword. On the other hand, supplies were left in the control of Parliament, and the principle which John Hampden had vindicated nearly twenty years before was thus triumphantly formulated in writing.

The composers of the new Constitution also went some way

to meet the demand for franchise reform – not that they extended the franchise itself, but they improved the decrepit borough system. They disfranchised many small boroughs and filled up the places in Parliament by allotting a larger number of Members to the counties, the numbers being graded according to size. This arrangement was in reality little more than a sensible acknowledgment of what had already long been the case. The lesser boroughs returned country gentlemen as often as not, the sons and relations of the landowning gentry. The same gentlemen now entered Parliament, as it were, in their true colours, with no further pretence to being the deputies of towns rather than of country districts. The Honourable Member for East Retford, for instance, became one of the Honourable Members for Nottinghamshire. The only important alteration was the creation of two new boroughs, the rising towns of Leeds and Halifax.

On 16 December, 1653, Cromwell was installed as Protector at Westminster Abbey. It was a simple ceremony, Cromwell himself being dressed in plain black velvet. For the moment the country was calm and the new Government to all outward appearances popular.

The Genoese agent, writing to inform his masters that the Protector was an ally worth courting, recognised a political fact to which Cromwell still tried to close his eyes – that he, Oliver Cromwell, was the pillar on which alone the State rested.

What was the actuality and what the theory of Cromwell's position? By the *Instrument of Government* he held his power under Parliament, and could govern independently only when Parliament was not sitting, all his actions being subject ultimately to the veto of that assembly. He was bound to consult them at frequent intervals because financial control was in their hands, and they were to make an even harsher use of this power than Cromwell anticipated. This, then, was the theory – not dictatorship, but a monarchy more strictly limited by statute than that of the Stuarts.

However, as commander-in-chief of the Army, Cromwell had a greater power of physical coercion than any Stuart. But – and herein lay another, and this time unparliamentary, check on the Protector's power – how far could he rely on his Army? The Levellers had been quelled, but among the most influential officers there were many whose views were far more emphatically republican than Cromwell's. He could not afford to offend these men, or at least not all of them, and unless he could trim his policy to please both them and Parliament, he would find himself deserted both by military force and economic assistance in his hour of need.

Cromwell acted throughout with the advice and assistance of a Council which he dominated but could not disregard. Here, too, there was latent opposition of another sort – from one ambitious officer at least, who sat at the Council table meditating whether he was not a wiser man than the Protector. This was the grave-faced general whom Cromwell called 'bottomless Lambert' because he could not plumb his secrets, or in happier moods, when he sought to bury his mistrust in a partly genuine affection, his 'dear Johnny.'

One other check controlled Cromwell's authority – his own theories. Events forced a power upon him which he was nothing loth to take, since he believed that he would use it well. But he was no natural revolutionary and he valiantly disregarded what was revolutionary in his situation. In his own mind he was always a 'poor gentleman that asks nothing better than to serve the public', or, as he even more graphically described it, a constable paid to keep the peace in an unruly parish. In his political theories he was for ever groping his way back towards the normal. If he contemplated changing the title of 'Protector' for that of 'King' it was principally because the title of 'King' was the more traditional. He believed sincerely in Parliamentary government: to have ceased to believe in it would have been to admit that he had fought two wars for nothing, that young Oliver and young Walton and so many others had died in vain. Yet below all this brave pretence, he realised the hopelessness of attempting a permanent settlement. He could not, on that account, abandon the principles for which he had striven and on which he had once hoped that a settlement might be made.

His attitude to personal liberty remained always the same in theory. He held that 'it was an unjust and unwise jealousy to deprive a man of his natural liberty upon a supposition he may abuse it : when he doth abuse it, judge.' Unhappily, Cromwell's subjects and Parliaments were all too much given to the abuse of their natural liberty, as he saw it. He was to be for ever judging.

Cromwell was not personally ambitious, or at least not inordinately so. Those who upbraided him with this vice misunderstood both the man and the situation. He was certainly granted great possessions, for he owned six or seven palaces and kept great state at Whitehall. But could he have done less? The modern taste for simplicity in rulers was foreign to the social outlook of that time. An ascetic indifference to honours would not much have impressed the seventeenth century, and would not have served to strengthen Cromwell's power. Disregard for social distinction had no place in his nature. The example in the flouting of privilege set by the Levellers in politics, and by the Quakers in social life, met with relatively little sympathy or admiration from contemporaries.

Cromwell as an obscure MP speaking in the House of Commons in a badly cut home-spun suit would pass : Cromwell fulfilling the duties of a sovereign in an ill-made suit would not have passed at all; the position demanded a careful outward dignity. There is no humour in Sir Philip Warwick's grave account of the improvement in his manners and attire when he came to rule over England. The thing was absolutely necessary. Necessary, too, was the formality of Whitehall, the grave investitures, the obsequious courtesies before the throne, the bare heads of men who had once been his fellow-officers, and the introduction of 'Your Highness' as the correct form of address. Republicanism at this time bore no necessary connection with a lesser formality and respect for authority: the Court of the Dutch Republic was famous as the most formal in Europe and the Doge of Venice kept great state.

His old mother, always in a flutter for her boy's safety, and his elderly wife did their best in the circumstances. They made it all faintly ridiculous. So also did the daughters, enormously and frankly enjoying their role as princesses. But it was not the assumption of regal formality which struck malicious critics: rather it was the failure to assume it easily. When the Protector asked for an orange to squeeze over his roast mutton – his favourite sauce – the Lady Protectress shouted out that oranges were a groat a-piece and he must do without: so the story. It is improbable that Mrs Cromwell so far forgot herself, but the circulation of such tales is eloquent of the impression which she made, poor thrifty soul, after a life of sparing and contriving, called suddenly to plod heavy-footed in the halls where the trim French Queen had danced.

Even for his children Cromwell showed very little ambition. Only under strong persuasion did he appoint his able younger son Henry Lord Deputy of Ireland, and he did not give his elder son Richard even that training in politics which he should have had. His two elder daughters had been married before the war ended, Elizabeth at sixteen to John Claypole, a Northamptonshire landowner, and Bridget to Henry Ireton. After his death in 1651 she married another of her father's officers, Charles Fleetwood. Neither Henry nor Richard married into the nobility and if the younger girls did better than their sisters they did not do so well as contemporaries had expected. Mary was given to the Yorkshire peer, Lord Fauconberg, and Frances threw herself, with a determination that broke down her father's objections, into the arms of the Earl of Warwick's heir. Cromwell clearly thought less of founding a dynasty than of settling his children respectably in case of untoward events after his death. In this he was successful : not one of them but died in comfortable circumstances and on English soil. Even Richard who had succeeded him, briefly, as Protector was able to return in the end from exile and live quietly under another name. Cromwell's long-surviving wife found a peaceful home with her son-in-law, the bluff and hearty Claypole.

At the time of his elevation to the Protectorate, Cromwell was approaching fifty-five years of age, which was not young for the seventeenth century. In fact he was the oldest effective ruler in Europe. The King of Spain and the Emperor were each seven or eight years his junior, although both considered themselves past the prime of life. The Grand Pensionary of Holland, John de Witt, was less than thirty; so was the Queen of Sweden. The nearest to Cromwell in age was the chief Minister of the French Crown, Cardinal Mazarin, and even he was three years younger. Moreover, few men in the seventeenth century held positions such as Cromwell now occupied without passing through years of practical political training. All the training Cromwell had had in the art of government had been gained in a few sessions of Parliament and in the local politics of a quiet English county. His civil government, like his soldiering, was to be unorthodox.

The Protectorate began with eight months of unimpeded rule by Cromwell and his Council of State, during which time the new Government more than justified its existence. Cromwell's first care was for the unification of the three kingdoms, an ambitious scheme which worked comparatively well during his lifetime and foreshadowed developments only to be fully realised two generations later. He decreed that both Scotland and Ireland should send representatives to Parliament at Westminster, Scotland being ruled under his authority by General Monck, Ireland first by his son-in-law, Fleetwood, and later by his son, Henry Cromwell. His plans for the internal government of Scotland were genuinely enlightened : he swept away oppressive feudal jurisdictions, privileges and servitudes and encouraged trade with England. His measures, combined with the firm and intelligent management of George Monck, restored peace and a measure of prosperity to the land and won some mournful praise even from the Scots.

Cromwell's Irish policy, on the other hand, was based on a total ignorance of Irish history, on blind resentment of the rebels who had so nearly overthrown English rule, and a fanatical determination to make an end of popery. He had also an army to satisfy and a revenue to raise. In the worst possible sense, it was a bold policy – in theory, in execution and in effect wholly bad – for Cromwell aimed at nothing less than settling the Irish question once and for all, by stamping out the Catholic Church and penning the native population into the inland parts of Connaught and Clare. Confined to these districts, the original inhabitants of the island would be cut off from the English settlers by the bogs and the River Shannon, and from the rest of the world by the sea. In theory the plan had a kind of brutal genius : in fact it could not be carried out. Irish landowners could be driven out and repatriated forcibly in their allotted counties, but no English settler would take over land unless he could be certain of a peasantry to work it for him. Thus the Irish remained as a subject race in the lands which Cromwell's settlers and soldiers took from the native owners.

In all, Cromwell's confiscations affected more than half the land in Ireland, 11 million acres : of these 3 million were worthless bog and something over a million were granted back to the Irish in Clare and Connaught. Cromwell thus had about 6 million acres, a third part of the habitable land in the country, to divide among the settlers. About 6,000 landowners were totally deprived of their possessions, and some 30,000 Irishmen became exiles, not counting those others – whose number also ran into a few thousands – whom Cromwell had transported to Barbados. The immense upheaval, the political consequences and individual injustices of this system can hardly be overestimated.

At the end of the war Cromwell promised amnesty to all the Irish not guilty of the murder of English settlers. The interpretation of the word 'murder' in a country which had long been in the anarchy of civil war may cover a wide field. Cromwell's ruling could have condemned thousands of Irishmen to death. In fact about two hundred were executed. Active co-operation with the English was taken as the only criterion by which the right of a landowner to preserve his estates could be judged, a ruling which bore hard against minors, women and the unfit, whose quiescence in the revolt placed them by default among the rebels. The Catholic faith was altogether prohibited and all priests expelled. Fortunately the banishment order was laxly carried out, and the actual execution of priests came to an end with the war itself. In some ways indeed the proscribed faith was little if at all worse off than under Stuart rule: proscription was at least no new thing. The internment camps for priests on the Arran islands are an early example of this method of dealing with the opponents of government, but had no effect whatever in extinguishing the faith of the Irish people.

The best that can be said for Cromwell's rule is that he established order after a decade of chaos. In the context of the Protestant politics of his time he was doing what he could to redeem a people corrupted and misled. In the unforgiving perspective of history his Irish policy did an ill service to England and to Ireland irreparable wrong.

In England, meanwhile, Cromwell took steps to improve moral and secular education. Ministers of religion were now appointed by a central committee, with local committees to see that they performed their duties conscientiously. He encouraged the propagation of the Gospel in the wilder regions of Wales and the neglected and barren parts of the country, and allowed freedom to sectarian preachers unless their teaching became a danger to the public peace. The Episcopal Church of England was no longer recognised; it had been forbidden under the Long Parliament. But the expropriated Bishops and deprived clergy often continued to hold services in private houses and in general the government turned a blind eye to their actions. The same held good for Roman Catholics who were better off under Cromwell than they had been during the Civil War, let alone in the reign of Elizabeth I.

A beginning was made in the extension of higher education. Grants were made for the help and maintenance of schools and teachers. Plans were considered for the foundation of a new college at Oxford and a new University for the North, at Durham. Cromwell was also a benefactor to learned institutions. His name stands next to that of Archbishop Laud on the tablet which commemorates the benefactors of the Bodleian Library at Oxford, and he is remembered at the University of Glasgow along with Mary Queen of Scots, Montrose and Argyll.

The traditional idea of Cromwell's rule as a time of austerity requires modification, and some at least of the austerity was the outcome of a difficult political situation rather than of Puritanism. While the regulations against duelling, cock-fighting and swearing were in some degree actuated by moral considerations, the ordinances against horse-racing, the proliferation of ale-houses and even against the theatre were chiefly intended to prevent the concourse of large numbers of people among whom riot and disturbances might break out.

Cromwell was himself fond of country sports and seriously interested in improving the breed of horses. There is no direct evidence that he disapproved of racing and his son-in-law John Claypole was a great promoter of it.

He was a lover of music though his taste did not extend to Church music, beyond the singing of psalms. Like most Puritans he felt that elaborate music in Church was a distraction from worship, rather than a help to it. But there was much music-making at his Court at Whitehall and vocal and instrumental concerts often formed a part of the entertainment offered to ambassadors. In 1656 he relaxed the ban on the theatre, and gave Davenant permission to produce at Drury Lane musical dramas on suitable subjects. The first of these was a propaganda piece showing the English liberating the people of Peru from the tyranny of Spain. It coincided, of course, with the war on Spain.

There could be no return to the international culture in the visual arts which had distinguished the Court of Charles I. The King's magnificent collection had been sold as one of the first acts of the Commonwealth to help defray the costs of the war. The great collection of the Duke of Buckingham had been dispersed to pay the fines incurred by his son as a Cavalier. Great foreign painters no longer came to England. Although a lesser German portraitist, Peter Lely, was gradually building up his reputation in London, English talent was now in demand. Robert Walker became the most successful portrait painter of the decade and left us at least one impressive picture of Cromwell in a pose imitated from Van Dyck. More distinguished was the miniaturist Samuel Cooper, an artist of real sensibility. The fine engraver William Faithorne, who had begun to make his name among the Cavaliers, did well during the Protectorate by replacing the faces of eminent Royalists in his beautiful plates by those of eminent Cromwellians. Lastly a word should be said of the coinage and medals issued under Cromwell, distinguished by an impressive clarity of design, the work of Thomas Simon.

In civil government Cromwell attempted at least to carry out some of the reforms which had been hoped for when he came to power. He appointed new judges and passed ordinances for the relief of debtors and for the reduction of legal charges to the poor. He was anxious to reform the Court of Chancery, but here his efforts failed because of the dogged opposition of the lawyers.

He failed not merely with Chancery but with the criminal code, which he regarded as too harsh and would willingly have altered. He felt, as we saw, that capital punishment was too frequently inflicted. His views were typical of his practical, generous, yet illogical approach to legal subjects. He would gladly have spared the petty thief, but he was willing, if need be, to fly in the face of English tradition and to refuse traitors the right of trial by jury, when he thought that he might not secure a conviction. In 1654 Gerard and Vowell were denied trial by jury when they were condemned to death for a plot against his life, and the Royalist Mordaunt appealed in vain for a jury four years later. Nevertheless, if Cromwell was prepared in an emergency to override the provisions made by English law for the protection of the accused, he genuinely desired more constructive and humane legislation.

He was more fortunate in his efforts towards administrative reform. He inherited from the Long Parliament an admirable Secretary of State in John Thurloe. This exceptionally gifted man was able to draw the threads of administration together into his hands and to train an efficient staff. The tradition which ascribes the formation of the British Civil Service to Cromwell is basically sound. Half-way through his reign we find the rapacious Clerks of the Privy Seal and Signet loudly lamenting that their fees and perquisites have disappeared and imploring the Protector to guarantee them instead a reasonable salary. It is the dawn of a great reformation.

John Thurloe's other achievement was the creation of an efficient secret service, of inestimable help to the Protector in gauging the feelings of his own country and in directing his foreign policy. For his Latin Secretary, that is, for composing official letters to foreign powers, Cromwell employed John Milton, who was assisted in his office by yet another poet, Andrew Marvell.

In foreign affairs the brief reign which was to be so aggressively glorious opened with a more pacific policy. War with the United Provinces, beginning in 1652, had for some months past grievously strained the resources of the Government. Cromwell's first act was to end hostilities which he had never himself desired. The young Grand Pensionary of Holland, John de Witt, was equally anxious for peace. The Dutch, who had expected an easy victory, had been taken aback by the spirit of the Commonwealth Navy and the skill of its commanders, chief among them Robert Blake. Terms were concluded without delay. The Dutch guaranteed the security of her commerce in the East Indies, agreed to make good the losses previously suffered by English merchants, conceded the supremacy of the English flag in the Narrow Seas and swore to exclude the House of Orange, close kin to the House of Stuart, for ever from their government.

At the same time, in the spring of 1654, Cromwell signed favourable commercial treaties with Portugal and Sweden, and a few months later came to an agreement with Denmark by which the Sound was thrown open to English shipping. Thus in a few months he had laid the basis of a fundamentally peaceful policy of alliances with the Protestant Powers, founded on community of commercial, political and religious interest.

With these achievements already behind him, Cromwell opened his first Parliament on 3 September, 1654, the anniversary of his victories at Dunbar and Worcester. In a speech full of hope, he placed the ratification of his powers by the *Instrument of Government* in their hands. 'Gentlemen,' he began; 'you are met here on the greatest occasion that, I believe, England ever saw: having upon your shoulders the interests of three great nations.' He ended by urging them 'to a sweet gracious and holy understanding of one another and of your business.'

The composition of the House to which Cromwell made his appeal was only in part different from that of its two predecessors. Half of its members – the most experienced and vocal half – had sat in Parliament before and were well acquainted with all the methods whereby their power could be asserted and maintained.

The first trouble was likely to come – and did come – from the Republicans who objected to the *Instrument of Government* for giving a king-like power to Cromwell. Their attack on the *Instrument* was an attempt to demolish it rather than to amend it, and as such seemed to threaten the stability of the state. Cromwell intervened to insist that Parliament take the *Instrument* as the basis of discussion. At this many of the Republicans withdrew. But those who remained demanded that the safeguards on Parliamentary power – that power for which the war had been fought – were insufficient. The supremacy of Parliament was no real supremacy unless they, and not Cromwell, had the ultimate control over the Army. It was the very right for which they had first made war on King Charles. But how could it be conceded now, by a Protector who was entirely dependent on the Army for his authority and position in the State?

Calculating that Cromwell would not dissolve them until they had granted supplies, for he had no legal right to raise money without them, the Commons imagined that they were safe. They reckoned without the Protector. He let them sit to the limit of the time prescribed for Parliaments by the *Instrument of Government* – five months, and he made them lunar, not calendar, months! – and then dissolved them. It is easy to understand what prompted his action : his Government, stable during the period of his independent rule, was gravely shaken by the behaviour of his Parliament. Thinking his rule insecure, the Royalists believed that there was a chance for their King, the Levellers for their republic.

Cromwell knew the gravity of the situation and saw in the resumption of personal control the best way to restore confidence. 'The people will prefer their safety to their passions and their real security to forms,' he said; he had now openly taken the formula of *salus populi suprema lex* for his own.

But the situation was still dangerous. Parliament was dissolved on 22 January, 1655. In the early spring the Levellers began to raise their heads once more. Cromwell did what he could to conciliate such of them as did not directly threaten his Government. After an interview with George Fox, he allowed the Quaker movement to gather momentum unmolested. Not from Quakers but from Anabaptists and Fifth Monarchy Men came the real danger.

More serious was the Royalist revolt in Wiltshire, which broke out in March under the leadership of John Penruddock. Immediate and widespread arrests of Royalists, followed by confiscations and civil penalties, quelled the Cavaliers. The Genoese agent estimated that the Protector had deprived four-fifths of the old ruling class of their privileges. The exaggeration was significant in so far as it reflected the resentful quiescence of the Royalists.

Unsupplied by Parliament, Cromwell naturally used this revolt to raise more money for his Government. Apart from the new confiscations, he imposed a capital levy of a tenth, a 'decimation,' on the Royalists, out of which he defrayed the cost of a new form of military rule imposed on the country. He divided England into districts, each to be controlled by a Major-General who was to see to the execution of Government ordinances, to keep a register of the inhabitants of their districts and to record their comings and goings, and, strange confusion of moral and police measures, to 'promote godliness and virtue' by all means in their power. They had authority to break up public meetings, to close ale-houses and to search dwellings.

The rule of the Major-Generals marks the high point of Cromwell's use of military force to secure his Government. For the time-being he had been driven to abandon his hopes of general conciliation and to rely not only on the threat of force but on a system of spies and intelligencers (well organised by Thurloe who had infiltrated all the Royalist organisations).

By the summer of 1655 his rule was almost as tyrannous – and far more unpopular – than that of Henry VIII had been more than a hundred years before.

But he accepted the situation only as a temporary phase. Though he did at times break out with angry words and declare that the people were unfit to be governed except by coercion, he never for long lost sight of the better government that he hoped to create and the receding liberties in which he still sincerely believed. The rule of the Major-Generals was brought to an end after eighteen months.

Driven by monarchical revolt to abandon his policy of conciliation, Cromwell was driven by republican revolt to curtail his policy of toleration. Plots and risings among Levellers and sectaries forced him to limit his previous concessions and arrest the leaders of the sects, among them his old comrade in arms, Thomas Harrison.

He was having increased opposition from the law. Whitelocke and Widdrington resigned as a protest against his meddling with Chancery. Two judges, Newdigate and Thorpe, refused to carry out his policy against Royalist rebels in the north. When a merchant named Cony refused to pay his Customs dues, denying the validity of the new Constitution, Cromwell called upon Lord Chief Justice Rolle to defend the legality of the dues, and Rolle also resigned his office.

Unable to reconcile Royalists or Republicans, deserted by many of his old comrades, accused of ambition by men who had once been his friends, Cromwell was only saved from bitter disillusion by his continuing faith in God. So long as the Army was loyal his Government was in itself secure. But it was not the Government he had hoped for. It rested on force, it had failed to secure the liberties for which he himself had fought, and it had no future beyond his death. Bitterly he wrote to his son-in-law, Fleetwood, in the summer of 1655: 'The wretched jealousies that are amongst us and the spirit of calumny turn all into gall and worm-wood.'

EIGHT

Foreign Policy
1655-1658

THE troubles at home that had marked the year 1655 were more than counter poised by Cromwell's successes abroad. Although he had failed to achieve the political peace of England for which he had hoped, the princes and statesmen of Europe regarded him as the strongest ruler that England had had for many years. Only an extraordinary man could have risen from such small beginnings to hold sway over three nations. For the last fifty years they had felt neither respect nor fear for any King of England, but they respected and feared this formidable upstart and had good reasons for doing so. He commanded an Army which had been everywhere victorious and a Navy which had recently held its own against the Dutch, who had been for many years the greatest sea-power in the world. Cromwell's navy was especially significant because England without sea-power was negligible in European diplomacy.

Charles I had built ships, but he had failed to create an effective navy. Things had begun to change in the Civil War. Soon after Naseby Parliament embarked on a business-like ship building plan, and shortly after the King's death Popham, Blake and Deane were put in charge of the fleet. All three had served with distinction as soldiers in the wars, and all three had also had some naval experience in their earlier lives. Popham and Deane were both good commanders. Blake is one of the greatest in the long roll of great English admirals.

Thus from the beginning of the Protectorate Cromwell disposed of strong military and naval power. No previous ruler of England had had well-organised naval and military forces on this scale permanently at his command, nor had any English sovereign held both Scotland and Ireland in subjection. It was true that Cromwell's position was vulnerable to conspiracy at home if a determined foreign power thought it worth while to stimulate such a thing (as foreign powers had done against Elizabeth I) but most of Cromwell's contemporary rulers preferred his alliance to any scheme for restoring the Stuarts. Great Britain, which had been of very little importance in Europe under the late King, was now — to the disgust and dismay of exiled Royalists — a significant and much courted power under the usurper.

Cromwell rose to the opportunity. Once again he showed his innate sense and judgment in an unfamiliar situation. Yet he had no training in foreign affairs and his past experience, such as it had been, was largely misleading. He had grown up during the years of national retrogression which followed the Elizabethan age. As a young man he had shared the impotent resentment felt by a majority of the Protestant gentry at the foreign policy of King James I. He had watched the defeat of the Protestant cause in Europe by the powerful Spanish-Austrian Habsburg alliance. English volunteers had fought in the Protestant armies but the English government intervened ineffectively, or remained neutral, or courted Spain. Cromwell, bringing his religious preoccupations into foreign policy as into all other spheres, still applied the phrases of his youth to explain his actions and spoke in terms applicable to the religious wars of the last century, though religion as a motive force had died in the bloody confusion of the Thirty Years War.

His religious fervour often sounded out of date among the secular calculations that governed contemporary diplomacy, but his policy belonged to the modern world of commercial rivalries and expanding opportunity. When he set himself to build a Protestant alliance in Europe he was thinking as much of Baltic trade and the balance of power as of religion. He understood perfectly that Catholic France was the natural ally against Catholic Spain. One of his first treaties was made with Portugal, another Catholic power, but in revolt against Spain. He drove a hard bargain, giving the valuable friendship of England in return for freedom to trade in all Portuguese overseas possessions, Brazil, the West Indies, Africa and India. During the negotiations the Portuguese ambassador's brother killed an Englishman in a street brawl. In spite of urgent protests from the embassy diplomatic immunity was refused, and the young man was tried and executed. The ambassador signed the treaty on the morning of the execution.

The attack on Spain in the West Indies, which was the culmination of Cromwell's policy, was a trading war undertaken to establish English outposts and English influence in a region where Spain had long held the monopoly. Cromwell was perfectly aware of this, but he also believed that any extension of English power must be acceptable to God because it would bring the light of the Gospel to regions darkened by Popish idolatry and the smoke of the Inquisition.

Cromwell, like most men of his age and background, had an idealised image of Queen Elizabeth I and her resistance to the might of Spain. But his policy was not the same as hers. She had fought a defensive war and the attacks of her adventurous seamen had been private enterprise piracy. Cromwell's attack when it came was state policy with all the power of the state behind it, designed not to 'singe the King of Spain's beard' but to establish a rival claim to the trade and the oceans of the world.

Sea-power was Cromwell's strongest weapon and he used it with an inspired boldness, so that by the end of his brief reign the English navy had established its position not only in the North Sea, the Channel and the Baltic but in the Mediterranean, the West Indies, and the African coasts.

Yet there were moments when he stood forth as the champion of oppressed Protestants, with their cause at heart and no particular advantage to be gained. In the summer of 1655 a wave of indignation swept over Protestant Europe against the cruelties of the Duke of Savoy towards a group of his subjects, the small community of the Vaudois in the Italian Alps. These harmless and pacific heretics were being systematically hunted out of their homes by French and Irish soldiery. Cromwell's moral indignation was both just and genuine. He started a public subscription for the Vaudois with a gift of £2,000; he protested in blistering language to the Duke of Savoy and to Cardinal Mazarin for conniving at the atrocity, and circularised the Protestant rulers of Europe in terms of fervent anger expressed in the elegant latin of John Milton. Milton poured out his own equally strong feelings in his famous sonnet:

Avenge O Lord thy slaughtered saints whose bones
Lie scattered on the Alpine mountains cold . . .

The effect of Cromwell's anger was immediate. Cardinal Mazarin at once withdrew the French soldiers from the Duke of Savoy and stopped the persecution. What happened in Savoy (a satellite state) was his affair not Cromwell's; but he was determined not to lose Cromwell's friendship, and perhaps no less determined to prevent him from assuming some kind of moral leadership in Protestant Europe.

The Protestant alliance, which Cromwell had in mind when he came to power and for which he began to lay the foundation by bringing the Dutch war to an end, never fully materialised. He was to learn from experience that the rivalries between the Baltic powers would prevent any permanent friendship. He sent Whitelocke as ambassador to Sweden and this fatherly diplomat persuaded Queen Christina to sign a treaty of alliance, but the belligerent character of her successor,

Charles X, brought all hope of agreement between the Northern powers to nothing.

In a less worldly sphere, Cromwell supported the efforts of John Dury, a Protestant idealist who had given his life to the work of reconciling the Lutheran and Calvinist powers. Cromwell supported Dury on a number of missions in North Germany and the Baltic. Little came of his devoted work for religious peace and toleration. But Dury was widely respected for his dedication to this hopeless cause and Cromwell, by supporting him, gave international and public proof of his concern for union and understanding.

Meanwhile the Navy under Blake had begun the essential task of putting down piracy, at first in the Channel and the western approaches where it had become a continual menace in the 1640s, with the Dunkirk pirates operating in conjunction with the Irish. Then, in the spring of 1655, Blake entered the Mediterranean, threatened the pirate stronghold of Tunis, and made a treaty with the Dey of Algiers. Here he ransomed all the English captives. Forty Dutch slaves, who swam out to the English ships pleading for rescue, were ransomed by subscription by the English sailors – the men whom they had been fighting only a year before.

Early in the New Year of 1655 a naval expedition had gone out to the West Indies under the joint command of William Penn, an experienced sailor, and Robert Venables, an officer who had seen much service in Ireland, as general of the land forces on board. This ambitious operation, intended to break the Spanish hold on the Caribbean, was called the Western Design in Cromwell's council. It had a long history.

The Spaniards not only controlled the West Indies trade, they also molested and captured any ships in Caribbean waters, whatever their destination. Ever since the peace made with Spain by James I in 1604 there had been malcontents in England who resented the curtailment of their opportunities and the threat to their ships, and who would willingly have carried on the war with Spain privately at their own expense, by some sort of piracy – the more respectable kind which was called 'privateering'.

During the reign of King Charles I a group of such men had founded, on one of the smaller Caribbean islands, which they called Providence, a colony intended as a base for English free-lance operations. The secretary of the Providence Company was John Pym, the leader of the Commons during the first years of the Long Parliament; the members of the Company included many of his Parliamentary associates and several kinsmen of Cromwell. The Providence settlement had been sacked by the Spaniards in 1640. Two years later a private expedition under Captain William Jackson had been sent out to investigate the damage and the prospects. The Western Design of Cromwell's government was in part based on Jackson's reports.

Cromwell's council was not unanimous in supporting the design. There had always been a Spanish party among merchants and traders. Anglo-Spanish trade, going back far into the middle ages, was an important element in English prosperity. This would be jeopardised by war with Spain. The question was whether the gain in world trade would be greater than the loss in the old traditional commerce.

On the Council, John Lambert seems to have been the spokesman of those who opposed the Western Design. But the majority were against him. Cromwell himself cited the religious argument to weight the scale in favour of the attack on Spain. 'God,' he said, 'has not brought us hither where we are, but to consider the work we may do in the world, as well as at home.'

In the commission made out for those in charge of the Design, he again emphasised the moral and religious motives. This expedition was sent to the Caribbean to relieve the hapless natives from 'the cruelty, wrongs and injustices done and exercised upon them by the Spaniards' and to liberate them from 'miserable thraldom and bondage both spiritual and civil and . . . to make way for the bringing in the light of the Gospel and power of true religion.'

Unfortunately the expedition of Penn and Venables did not live up to expectation. The commanders themselves quarrelled. The attack on Hispaniola, the largest of the islands, failed altogether. They sailed therefore to Jamaica and took possession of it instead. This was a valuable prize, but it did not suit Cromwell to appear to accept the failure at Hispaniola, the premature return of the expedition, or the openly bad relations of the two commanders. He sent them both to the Tower.

The subsequent importance of Jamaica in building up the wealth of England and its key position in the slave trade hardly bore out Cromwell's avowed intention of liberating the natives from bondage and shedding the pure light of the Gospel. Still, he cannot be held directly responsible for these later events.

When the attack on Hispaniola was reported in Spain the King instructed his ambassador in London to protest in the strongest terms. The ambassador, Alonso de Cardenas, was long experienced in English politics and had successfully weathered the Civil War, the King's execution and the Commonwealth. But he got no satisfaction from Cromwell for the Caribbean attack and found himself obliged to ask for his passport and quit the country.

There was now open war with Spain. The logical consequence was co-operation with Spain's principal enemy, France, now under the able guidance of Cardinal Mazarin. In this alliance the strength of Cromwell's army was as important as the strength of his navy. Mazarin agreed to hand over the port of Dunkirk (when it should be captured) as the price of military aid from Cromwell's famous troops in the struggle with the Spaniards in Flanders. This was the significant term of the alliance. For Cromwell was not blind to the fact that French power in Flanders would be no less a menace to England than Spanish power had been. But the existence of an English garrison at Dunkirk would be a guarantee against this danger. It was just over a hundred years since the English had lost Calais and thereby forfeited their long dominance of the Narrow Seas. The cession of Dunkirk would give them back what they had lost.

The joint victory of France and England against Spain was now inevitable. In April 1657 Blake surprised and destroyed the treasure fleet at Santa Cruz and seized the silver so urgently needed for the payment of Spanish troops in Europe. It was an action of great daring and brilliance which aroused wild enthusiasm in England, but Blake did not live to be welcomed and acclaimed. He died on his way home, within sight of Plymouth and was buried in solemn state in Westminster Abbey.

In the following year the French and English allies defeated the Spaniards in Flanders at the Battle of the Dunes, and nine days later Dunkirk was handed over.

Critics were later to say that Cromwell's policy of helping France against Spain had laid the foundations of the menacing power of Louis XIV which overshadowed Europe in the next generation. But Cromwell had made provision against the danger of an over-mighty France just across the Channel when he acquired possession of Dunkirk. Besides, England in his time was herself a formidable power, strong enough to impose a certain caution on an aggressive neighbour. After Cromwell's death these advantages were lost. Dunkirk was sold, the Army was disbanded, and the navy, though still strong, was wasted in ill-considered ventures and in fighting the Dutch. It was not Cromwell's policy that allowed the France of Louis XIV to become a threat to Europe, but the policy – or lack of it – of those who came after him.

Besides, the defeat of Spain was not merely a European event. It opened up the trade of the world to the free enterprise of other nations, especially the French and the English.

In a reign of less than five years Cromwell's achievement was astounding. He had by his wide-ranging naval strategy gone far to indicate the full significance of sea-power for creating the conditions of world-wide trade, and he had foreshadowed possibilities and principles of international intervention which were to be fully developed only in the nineteenth century.

NINE

The End
1656-1658

In the autumn of 1656 pressing financial need forced Cromwell once again to call Parliament. By modern standards, Cromwell's annual budgets of between 2 and 3 million pounds seem very small, nor were they large by contemporary European reckoning. But English public finance was hampered by an inadequate system of taxation, unequal to the widening needs of government. Small as Cromwell's budgets were, they were far larger than anything hitherto contemplated by English rulers. Exclusive of his household, on which he spent £50,000 – £20,000 less than the impoverished Charles I – the Civil List accounted for a sum of less than £200,000, while in 1654, a year of peace, the Army and Navy between them swallowed 2½ millions.

This would have been all very well if there had been adequate means for raising the money. Customs and excise, the monthly assessments imposed in time of war and maintained afterwards, semi-forced loans, sale and confiscation of goods, Spanish prizes – all were not enough to meet the mounting bills.

As the years went on, the credit of his Government sank at home. Two City merchants, both once Members of Parliament and men of great wealth, Vassell and Avery, were in prison for debt because they had been unable to redeem the great sums they had advanced to the Government. This was a poor encouragement to other City men. Another appeal to the Commons seemed the only way and in September, 1656, Cromwell opened his second Parliament.

Cromwell's success abroad had gained him some popularity although the fear of an expensive war with Spain had somewhat damped it. There were growing murmurs at the government's indebtedness. The rule of the Major-Generals was increasingly unpopular even among neutral and Puritan gentry. All told, it hardly seemed that this Parliament would be more amenable than its predecessor.

Cromwell, or more probably some of the soldiers on his Council, took no chances. The names on the returns were scrutinised and over 100 members were prevented from taking their seats.

Cromwell's opening address has come down to us in an imperfect form, but making allowances for errors of transcription, it was more repetitive and long-winded than his earlier speeches. There are clear signs of strain. Yet he believed intensely in his message to Parliament, and through them to the nation. The war on Spain, he urged, was a holy war, a war for 'the glory of God and his interest in the world'. He reminded them of the past history of Spain, of persecutions, massacres and the Inquisition, and of the Spanish-contrived plots against 'Queen Elizabeth of famous memory'. He drew attention to the present protection accorded by Spain to the exiled Stuarts and to the plots against his own life.

Cavaliers and Papists were potential enemies in their midst. Recently they had drawn Leveller malcontents into their conspiracies. These things were true enough; he emphasised them to meet in advance the protests that he expected from Parliament against the Major-Generals. But the Major-Generals, he assured them, were 'instrumental to your peace and preservation'. No harm came to anyone who was content to live quietly; only Cavaliers and sectaries who refused to give any undertaking not to disturb the public peace were in trouble.

Several times he touched on the rising debts of the state. But he dismissed the popularly quoted figure of 2½ million as a great exaggeration. Debts there certainly were, but they had been incurred in the pursuit of God's work and the national interest. His government had been frugal and uncorrupt, he and his council had 'with honest and plain hearts laboured and endeavoured the disposal of treasure to public uses'. The claim was just; the Protectorate government was singularly free of peculation or self-seeking.

The great business before Parliament, he reiterated, was the war on Spain – Spain, which God himself had clearly indicated in the Scriptures, as head of the anti-Christian and Papal faction. His audience no doubt found it easier than we do to detect the passages in Thessalonians and Revelation which he had in mind as prophetic of the Anglo-Spanish conflict of 1656. And so he urged them to vote supplies in order that England might carry out her God-given mission against Spain. 'If Pope and Spaniard and Devil and all set themselves against us . . . yet in the name of the Lord we should destroy them.'

Parliament failed to respond to this clarion call. They wanted first an end to the rule of the Major-Generals. The alternative was a strengthened civil authority, a reformed and limited monarchy with Cromwell at its head. This was the last turn in the long contest between Parliament and Army, in which so far Parliament had had the worst of it. Cromwell, who knew how much his own power – whether he was called Protector or King – depended on his support by the Army, played for time.

Parliament certainly behaved as though there was time enough. The voting of supplies towards the Spanish war was hardly treated as urgent. Early in December public business was interrupted by a blasphemy case which Parliament, on no very clear grounds, took out of the civil courts into their own hands.

The culprit, a Quaker mystic named James Nayler, had a noble, ascetic face not unlike the popular conception of Christ.

His adherents, mostly women, had staged a humble imitation of the Entry into Jerusalem when they led him into Bristol, mounted on an ass, and waved leafy branches before him. Nayler asserted that they had only saluted him on account of that part of Christ which is in every man; he made no claim to *be* Christ. But his mystical and insubordinate answers at his trial incensed Parliament. Eighty-two members voted for the death sentence; by a majority of fourteen he was allowed to live, but only just. A savage penalty of three whippings and pillories was to be inflicted, followed by close imprisonment.

The case took over a week of Parliament's time. On Christmas Day Cromwell intervened. His reasons were in part humanitarian – some of Nayler's friends had appealed to him – but his letter to Parliament merely asked on what grounds they had taken the case into their own hands. The message had no effect on the fate of Nayler, who survived his punishment and in whose subsequent fate Cromwell was still interesting himself over a year later. All that happened at the time was that Parliament postponed a debate on the Spanish war for a long day's argument on the more congenial topic of their constitutional right to call offenders to account.

A few days later the discovery of a plot against Cromwell's life by the half crazy Leveller, Miles Sindercombe, jolted Parliament into a belated recognition that he was irreplaceable and deserved the only vote of confidence that it was in their power to give, namely, the supplies he had asked for.

Cromwell too understood the Parliamentary game; his personal supporters in the House, including his son-in-law Claypole, had for some time past opposed the militia bill, put forward by the Army group on the Council for raising money to support the Major-Generals. If this bill failed to pass, the Major-Generals were doomed. On 29 January it was rejected. This meant the collapse of their power through lack of funds; after just over a year and a half the unpopular military control of regional government was thus brought to an end. On the following day Parliament voted £400,000 for the Spanish war.

The Nayler case had started some serious thought in Parliament on the constitutional issue. This was further stimulated by the defeat of the Army party over the Major-Generals, indicating as it did Cromwell's own distaste for further government by force. The outcome was the draft constitution of a reformed monarchy, the *Humble Petition and Advice,* by which Parliament offered to make Cromwell King.

Though he had abandoned the Major-Generals, Cromwell was well aware that he could not further offend the susceptibilities of his followers in the Army. He needed Army support for the Spanish war, among other things. He had troops serving in alliance with the French. He had long since lost the confidence of the Republicans who had been his comrades in arms, such men as Ludlow and Harrison. Recently he knew he had lost the support of John Lambert, who had opposed the Spanish war and defended the Major-Generals. He could not afford to alienate those in the Army who still held to him, but who would turn from him if he should accept the title of King with all that it implied of personal and family ambition. After a month's political hesitation, he refused the Crown on 7 May, 1657. After that the *Humble Petition and Advice* lost much of its point. The document which procured the Protector's sanction on 25 May was comparatively insignificant. Cromwell was given power to nominate his successor, and a month later he was again installed as Lord Protector under the new Constitution, with greater pomp than before. John Lambert, who was openly opposed to these proceedings, was relieved of his place on the Council.

After the summer recess Parliament met again in January, 1658. In the meantime Cromwell had selected a number of men, some of them Members of Parliament, to form the Upper, or 'Other', House, which was the only other significant innovation in the new Constitution. Thus, when Parliament met, the Commons were denuded of his ablest supporters. Worse still, the 100 members excluded by his Council when Parliament first met had taken their seats under the new Constitution. Cromwell was now to find that the civil authority had not learnt better manners from its long suppression. Grievances, the Commons began aggressively, must be redressed before they could grant any more supplies. It seemed that the sum voted in the summer had already been engulfed in the wars. This placed them in a very strong position. The next move of the Lower House was to initiate an acrimonious argument with Cromwell's 'Lords' as to whether or not they really were 'Lords.'

Cromwell felt that there was nothing to be gained by prolonging this kind of session. Thirty years' experience of Parliaments had taught him what it would lead to. Rumours of plots, unearthed by the indefatigable Thurloe, gave him his excuse to be rid of the assembly, supply or no. If he had to call Parliament again he would probably be luckier, and he could hardly be less lucky, if he started with a fresh election. Fifteen days after opening the session, on 4 February, 1658, Cromwell came down to the House in a towering passion and for the third time in five years forcibly dissolved the representatives of the people. 'Let God be judge between you and me!' he stormed, the last words of his which were to ring out in an assembled Parliament.

He must have recognised then, and finally, that he had not solved the problems for which the war had been fought, and after the final dissolution of his second Parliament he seems to have abandoned all hope of doing so.

Not in this sphere is to be found the greatness of Cromwell's civil government. Yet it would be unfair to say that because he failed to solve the problems for which the war had been fought, he failed altogether. He gave England five years of security and comparative prosperity after long travail: he made possible by his measured and unvindictive, if stern, handling of the Royalists a calm and almost bloodless return to the monarchy. This latter was naturally not his intention, but this should not derogate from his merit in causing it. And again, in spite of the political pressure which prevented his measures from taking effect, he established for the imitation of future ages a standard of toleration. Although he did not allow Catholic worship, he did not penalise Catholics for not attending the religious worship authorised by the State. In the main he recognised the right of every man to possess his soul in freedom, so long as his belief did not lead to anti-social conduct. He loathed the necessity of persecution, and that for this time and age was broad enough. His generous encouragement of the Quakers, in some ways the most extreme, as they were also the most constructive, of the new sectaries, was much to his credit.

Interesting too at this time was his encouragement of a project for giving a national home to the Jews in England. Although nothing came of this Biblical and idealistic vision, he re-admitted the Jews after more than three centuries of exclusion and gave them rights of residence and of worship which were subsequently confirmed by Charles II.

For his attempts to reform administration, for the relative honesty and efficiency of his rule, the country should have been grateful. Marred as were the five years of his government by the penalising of the Cavaliers, by the arrests of Levellers, Anabaptists, Fifth Monarchy Men, by the spy system and the rule of the Major-Generals, yet taken as a whole they were years of rest and recovery.

Finance was the weak part of Cromwell's administration, as it was of most European administrations at that time. He was to leave a debt of 2 million pounds, but his Government had aimed high; he had wanted better education for the people and better care for the poor. The social conscience was awake and at work even if the seventeenth-century philanthropist cared disproportionately more for the soul than the body.

But it was in the service of the state, above all, that Cromwell's government began a new tradition. His principal Secretary of State, Thurloe, was a man of exceptional ability and character, more able to co-ordinate and organise the various branches of the administration than any of the King's servants had been for the last fifty years. Moreover the crisis through which the nation had passed gave to the civil servants of the Commonwealth and Protectorate a direct responsibility for the continuation of civil government that their predecessors had not felt in the same way. They had been called 'the King's Servants' under the old regime. In the traditional fashion of England, they are 'On Her Majesty's Service' to this day. But it was in Cromwell's time that the personal bond gave way to the sense of public duty. The career of so notable a civil servant as Samuel Pepys in the reign of Charles II represented the new traditions of the Navy Office which had evolved in Cromwell's time.

There was no revolutionary change. The development grew out of need for stability and continuity not guaranteed by politics alone. There was no deliberate plan. Cromwell did not himself show great originality, and indeed in finance his natural conservatism led him, not only to restore the Exchequer in 1654, but to stereotype the questionable fiscal methods of his predecessors rather than to evolve any new and all-embracing scheme. Had he been a dictator, his short reign would seem, from the internal point of view, sadly disappointing, for a dictator can and should do much. The wonder with Cromwell was that, his resources and powers being so limited, he did anything at all.

At the dissolution of his last Parliament, Cromwell was already on the threshold of his sixtieth year. A life of unceasing physical exertion had undermined his health. He had been ill in Ireland and seriously ill in January, 1657, and again at the end of the year. In the meantime his recreations were still of that strenuous kind which had diverted his youth. In his lighter moments he had time to interest himself in agricultural and domestic matters, particularly in the breeding of horses. Once, in the autumn of 1654, when the six Barbary horses which he had been driving in Hyde Park took fright and bolted, he had to jump for his life. Beyond a bruise and a sprain, no serious injury resulted.

Throughout the year 1658 he seemed well enough to the casual observer, but at 59 he was already an old man and troubles began to weigh on him. He had never carried them lightly and the prolonged strain of 'wrestling with the Lord' over every decision was bound to wear him out in the end. His immense confidence was not of that kind which brings with it a buoyant light-heartedness under responsibility. He knew that he was right, but not without long preliminary struggles; once even it was alleged that he had striven so hard with the Lord in the privacy of his room that his tears trickled out under the door – a malicious piece of Royalist mockery, but based on the truth that he prayed with a vehemence and physical exertion which prostrated him.

His mother, whose steady devotion had supported him to the very height of his career, died soon after his elevation to power. Her body was laid far away from the quiet land where she had spent her youth and womanhood, far from the bones of her unambitious husband, in the vaults of Westminster Abbey – the first of the Cromwell family to intrude on those exclusive precincts.

At the end of 1657, within a week of each other, Cromwell's 'little wenches', Frances and Mary, now nineteen and twenty years old, were married with festivities which included a musical entertainment much like a masque, to young Robert Rich, grandson of the Earl of Warwick, and Lord Fauconberg. But Frances was left a widow within three months of her marriage. A far heavier blow to Cromwell was the death in August,1658, of Elizabeth Claypole, who died of cancer at the age of twenty-nine. The frivolous little hoyden Betty, with her unashamed Royalism, her sympathetic intervention for the vanquished, and her pretty ways, was the dearest of his children. It was an open secret that she could manage him when no one else could, although the casual attitude to politics which she shared with her brother Dick prevented her from playing any leading part in Court intrigue.

The summer had been marked abroad by the resounding victory in Flanders at the Battle of the Dunes and the cession of Dunkirk to England. It was marked at home by the explosion of one last unsuccessful Royalist conspiracy and by the gathering menace of financial collapse. The treasure taken at Santa Cruz had been used up, the situation in the Navy was critical and the Government's debts were rising towards the 2 million mark. Cromwell knew he would have to call another Parliament and had already made up his mind to do so when his daughter died.

This was on 16 August, 1658. From that day Cromwell's physical resistance crumbled. Later in the month he had recovered enough from a bad attack of colic and gout to venture out again into the fresh air. It must have been at this time that George Fox met him riding in Hampton Court Park and 'saw and felt a waft of death go forth against him : and when I came to him he looked like a dead man.'

The Protector was well enough to make his way back to Whitehall to his wife before the last relapse set in. After some days of restless fever, he died on the anniversary of his triumphs at Worcester and Dunbar, on 3 September at four in the afternoon.

In those last hours he uttered broken words of prayer, noted down and perhaps a little put together by those who waited at his bedside. 'Lord,' Cromwell had prayed in the intervals of sleep and fever, 'Lord . . . I may, I will come to Thee for Thy people. Thou hast made me, though very unworthy, a mean instrument to do them some good, and Thee service : and many of them have set too high a value upon me. . . . Lord, however Thou do dispose of me, continue and go on to do good for them. Give them consistency of judgment, one heart and mutual love: and go on to deliver them . . . and make the name of Christ glorious in the world. Teach those who look too much on Thy instruments to depend more upon Thyself. Pardon such as desire to trample upon the dust of a poor worm, for they are Thy people too.'

Rumours multiplied as Cromwell lay dying. Some said General Lambert would succeed him, as the best man in the Army and the strongest personality among all those who had fought in the war. Others were for Fleetwood, Bridget's husband. A third party suggested that Fairfax, still barely fifty years old, was to be brought out of retirement. A fourth and smaller party murmured the name of young Henry Cromwell. None of these succeeded. Richard Cromwell, at thirty-two, lazy, intelligent, good-natured, had been nominated by his father: Richard Cromwell succeeded.

Until the passing of the *Humble Petition and Advice* Cromwell had made no effort to found a dynasty, and even afterwards, when by a choice of successor the way had been thrown open to him, he had done very little towards it, so little that one is almost tempted to believe that he did not himself trust in the permanency of the Protectorate. There was a kind of fatalism about the choice of Richard. He had the negative moral virtue that he was not likely to make trouble, and the negative political advantage that his succession, unlike that of any of the others, would not precipitate a split in the country. The Cromwell family had no support as such. The Protector had sought no splendid alliances abroad and had not even thought out the marriages of his daughters with any idea of reconciling the dissident groups in England. The family now stood or fell by its own merits, and by its own merits it fell — not unwillingly. After the Restoration Richard naturally had to go abroad for some time, but, like all the rest of the family, he eventually died in England. None of them, not even Henry, achieved any further distinction save that of being pointed out in streets and public places as the children of Oliver Cromwell – with interest and awe rather than with abhorrence. Frances and Mary continued their undistinguished and not unhappy lives as ladies of society, Frances consoling herself for her husband's early death by marrying Sir John Russell. Their mother lived out her days in the restful atmosphere of an English country house, never, one imagines, much regretting the irksome splendours of Whitehall. She had been there but five years of a long life, the shortest time that she and her husband had lived anywhere except at St. Ives.

Much though not all of Cromwell's work died with him. His immediate service had been to stop civil strife in England and give her back unity and self-respect. His more permanent service was to strengthen and develop the spirit of religious enquiry and individualism among the English, which flowered into the ineradicable, indestructible, harsh, fertile, stubborn growth of Nonconformity. His reforms might be swept away by the cross-currents and changes of the Restoration. Fundamentally, the mark he had left on the English character remained.

His body, buried with great pomp in the Abbey, was disinterred two years later and hanged at Tyburn; the severed head was afterwards, in the gruesome custom of the time, displayed on the roof of Westminster Hall.

Many different estimates of his character and his aspirations have been made. In his last years he had often spoken bitterly, calling the people 'a many-headed beast, incapable of reason,' and declaring that the sword alone was the best argument. Yet, casting up such statements against others of a more generous kind, it is easy to see that even to the end he believed in some better foundation for government than mere force. He loved the people and felt his responsibility towards them, nor did he ever wholly lose touch with them. To them his last thoughts turned : for them he prayed.

Even that last prayer shows how little he believed in force

as a basis for government. In the twilight of consciousness he uttered the phrase which gives the key to all: 'consistency of judgment, one heart and mutual love' – the only foundation for the permanent society. Dying, he could be again the idealist and the Christian that he had been before and, in all those years of stress, had vainly striven still to be.

His career illustrates that problem which confronts statesmen in every epoch. Civil liberty is always a limited and partial thing, as much in the twentieth century as in the seventeenth. Such as it was, such as he conceived of it, he believed in it and fought for it. But the liberty of the victors was the oppression of the vanquished, and even the liberty he had won was not what he had hoped for.

He had his armour against this worst of disillusions – the discovery that the thing gained was not the same as the thing which had been fought for. He kept always, in all changes of fortune, his strong belief in the power and guidance of God. He never grew cynical, never abandoned the conviction that there was in politics and in life, a Right and a Wrong decision; never lowered his ideals to think in terms of the expedient and inexpedient. It was perhaps a colossal self-deception in a man who so often changed his actions and his policies to meet an ever-changing situation. Yet he saw in every new development, in every shift of the political balance, something which he took to be 'none other than the hand of God'.

For many years the word 'Regicide' blotted out his name from the roll of English heroes. Then, after a period of revived popularity and better understanding in the liberal nineteenth century, his reputation fell again in the twentieth when he was associated in the popular mind with the dictators of modern Europe, to whom he had almost no resemblance either in his character or in the nature of his power.

Yet always he re-emerges – a formidable and unique personality which left an indelible mark on the national character.

At the height of his reputation as a national hero, early in the twentieth century his statue was set up, rather incongruously, outside Parliament which he had so often expelled. His real monument is neither cast in bronze nor written in books, but enshrined rather in popular legend and historic memory: the sense of a great and enigmatic figure, a powerful influence on the fate of England, on whom for good or evil the final judgment has not yet been given.

Postscript
Cromwell in Perspective

I WROTE this short account of Cromwell in 1939 when I was young enough to face undaunted the task of compressing his life and personality within the space allotted to authors in Duckworth's then recently launched series of *Great* (but brief) *Lives*.

The present version is revised and in parts much re-written. In the 34 years which have gone by since it first appeared, massive research has been done on the Stuart period, and new material has come to light. Our knowledge has been broadened and enriched by the opening up of new veins of enquiry and the re-working of older ones.

Yet the personality of Cromwell remains enigmatic and his reputation changes – as it will continue to change – with the moral and political climate of the living world. In 1939 the shadow of the European dictatorships darkened his image and historians who still clung to the older liberal interpretation of him as a national hero in the evolution of English liberty were thrown on to the defensive. They were often concerned above all to show that the Great Protector had nothing in common with the Führer or the Duce. This produced a rather negative interpretation, emphasising what Cromwell was *not*, rather than what he *was*. This struck me very forcibly when I looked again at what I had written in 1939, and I have, I hope, in the present version adopted a more constructive and objective approach.

Some writers, on the other hand, thought that they could detect parallels between Cromwell and contemporary dictators. The late Professor Abbott, to whom all students of the period are in debt for his devoted scholarship and indefatigable perseverance in giving us *The Writings and Speeches of Oliver Cromwell* – even he allowed modern comparisons to affect his judgment of Cromwell's policy and character during the Protectorate.

The disparagement of Cromwell by analogy outlasted the War by more than a decade. Even in the tercentenary year of 1958 popular comment still emphasised Cromwell the Dictator above all else.

The atmosphere has changed. If Cromwell is not quite a national hero, he is generally recognised as a great figure in our history, the soldier-statesman who put an end to civil war, restored peace at home and respect abroad. But his career and his character remain controversial.

He was hard to understand even in his own day. How much harder then is it for us to reach the heart of his mystery, since we must approach him through a mist of prejudices, beliefs and received opinions very different from those of his own time.

Royalists and Anglicans saw him as an ambitious, bad man who laid sacrilegious hands on the sacred person of his King. Many who had once been his colleagues in Parliament and his comrades in arms came to hate and denounce him. Presbyterian Parliament-men, like Denzil Holles, execrated him for his tolerance and encouragement of the Independent sects and his championship of the Army against the House of Commons. Extreme sectaries, like Thomas Harrison, condemned him for substituting his own rule for the Rule of the Saints. Stalwart Commonwealth men, like Harry Vane and Edmund Ludlow, turned from him in disgust and disillusion when he betrayed the Republican ideal and became Protector. John Lilburne and the Levellers denounced him as a juggling knave who had brought to nothing their programme for a government more broadly based on consent, a reformed Parliament and a just society.

Among the great mass of Cromwell documents, only a small proportion reveal the private man: enough to indicate the melancholia that afflicted him in earlier years and the release which his conversion brought to him; enough to reveal the conscientious family man, anxious to settle his children in life, arranging their marriages in the intervals of war. We know, too, of outbursts of boisterous mirth and horseplay which seem out of key with his earnest nature – hurling a cushion at Ludlow, or throwing sweetmeats about at his daughter's wedding. Two or three incidents – and we know of no more – are perhaps hardly enough to suggest that this kind of thing was a habit.

There are more records of uncontrollable anger, always on occasions of great political tension. There may have been private rages, but we only know of public ones – and well-directed at that.

In anger or excitement, he could be almost incoherent, although in some of his public utterances it is fair to make allowance for the inefficiency of seventeenth-century reporting. His eloquence could at times be powerful, but it was the strength of his feelings that made it so. His natural, forthright use of words was often memorable, sometimes magnificent; but at other times, and especially in argument, his thoughts came too fast for his tongue and issued in broken, repetitive vehemence. His actions in crisis, whether on the battle-field, in Parliament or at the Council table, show a clear and bold judgment; but he was not good at analysing or presenting the reasons behind his actions. Prayer helped him towards all his considered decisions, and the insights which were then vouchsafed to him he took for direct revelation, rather than the outcome of his own thought below the level of conscious formulation.

In his years of power there is no evidence of any personal pleasure or even gratification at his own greatness: no evidence that ambition had been satisfied. Can this be taken as evidence that personal ambition was never a motive with him? I am inclined to think so.

He felt the burden but did not enjoy the rewards of his position. His personal joys and griefs came from his private feelings – grief for the loss of friends, for the fatal illness of his beloved daughter, and joy – more rarely – at moments of relaxation and family gaiety. As Protector he appeared, in spite of his power at home and prestige abroad, a sad and heavily burdened man.

His likeness, at the time of his rise to power, was taken once by a great and sensitive artist who could penetrate beyond the official facade. The young Samuel Cooper, in an unfinished miniature, tells us more of the real Cromwell than any document. The face is deeply serious, thoughtful and strong. But the eyes do not meet those of the spectator. This is a man who has seen all that he needs to see of the world and its politics, who will do, with God's help, what he believes has to be done. But it is the inward life alone which matters to him, the still centre of his undeviating trust in God.

Bibliographical Note (revised to 1973)

CARLYLE's *Letters and Speeches of Oliver Cromwell* was the pioneer treatment of his life in full; although out of date for purposes of modern study, it remains a classic in its own right. For the modern scholar W. C. Abbott's *Writings and Speeches of Oliver Cromwell,* four volumes, (Harvard, 1937-1951), is indispensible. Among the many contemporary memoirs which throw light on Cromwell those of Edmund Ludlow (edited by Sir Charles Firth) are the most important.

Cromwell's biography by Sir Charles Firth, first published in 1900, and re-issued in *The World's Classics* with an introduction by G. M. Young in 1953, still holds its own. Maurice Ashley in *Oliver Cromwell and the Puritan Revolution* (1958) and *The Greatness of Oliver Cromwell* (revised edition 1967) sympathetically assesses Cromwell's place in history in the light of modern research. His religious thought is carefully treated in R. S. Paul, *The Lord Protector: Religion and Politics in the Life of Oliver Cromwell* (1955). Christopher Hill in *God's Englishman: Oliver Cromwell and the English Revolution* (1970) analyses his ideas and actions in relation to the revolutionary changes of the seventeenth century and is especially good on his foreign policy.

For the military side Sir Charles Firth, *Cromwell's Army* (third ed. 1921) is essential. L. F. Solt, *Saints in Arms* (1959) is valuable for the religious influences on the troops. Austin Woolrych, *Battles of the English Civil War* (1961) is outstandingly good on Marston Moor and Preston. See also C. V. Wedgwood, *The King's War* (1959).

For the Navy, J. R. Powell, *The Navy in the Civil War* (1962) is a good account of a neglected subject and fills in the background to the naval revival under Cromwell. The same author's life of *Robert Blake* (1972) is also most valuable.

For Ireland, R. Dunlop, *Ireland under the Commonwealth* (1913) and T. J. Coonan, *The Irish Catholic Confederation and the Puritan Revolution* (1954); also Prendergast, *The Cromwellian Settlement in Ireland* (second edition, 1922). Special aspects of Cromwell's rule are dealt with by Maurice Ashley, *Financial and Commercial Policy under the Cromwellian Protectorate* and Menna Prestwich, 'Diplomacy and Trade in the Protectorate', *Journal of Modern History* (1950).

For the general history of the period the great work of S. R. Gardiner, completed by Sir Charles Firth, is still an invaluable guide. Maurice Ashley's volume on the Stuarts in the *Pelican History of England* Christopher Hill's *Century of Revolution* (1961) and Ivan Roots, *The Great Rebellion* (1966) interpret the problems of the period from the point of view of twentieth-century historical thought and with the benefit of much recent detailed research.

For the Levellers the best general work is H. N. Brailsford, *The Levellers and the English Revolution*, which was prepared for publication after his death by Chistopher Hill. (1961). For the religious and political thought of the period and especially for the ferment in the Army, see A. S. P. Woodhouse, *Puritanism and Liberty* (second edition, 1951) which contains the Army debates of 1647; and the richly documented volumes of Professor William Haller, *The Rise of Puritanism* (1938) and *Liberty and Reformation* (1955).

Recent works on special aspects include David Underdown, *Pride's Purge* (1971), C. V. Wedgwood, *Trial of Charles I* (1964) and a valuable collection of essays by foremost scholars in the period – *The Interregnum: the Quest for a Settlement 1646-1660* edited by G. E. Aylmer (1972). A full-length biography by Antonia Fraser is in the press.

Index

.